D0944533

The Observer's Pocket Series

EUROPEAN COSTUME

The Observer Books

A POCKET REFERENCE SERIES
COVERING A WIDE RANGE OF SUBJECTS

Natural History

BIRDS
BIRDS' EGGS
BUTTERFLIES
LARGER MOTHS
COMMON INSECTS
WILD ANIMALS
ZOO ANIMALS
WILD FLOWERS
GARDEN FLOWERS
FLOWERING TREES
  AND SHRUBS
HOUSE PLANTS
CACTI
TREES
GRASSES
COMMON FUNGI
LICHENS
POND LIFE
FRESHWATER FISHES
SEA FISHES
SEA AND SEASHORE
GEOLOGY
ASTRONOMY
WEATHER
CATS
DOGS
HORSES AND PONIES

Transport

AIRCRAFT
AUTOMOBILES
COMMERCIAL VEHICLES
SHIPS

MANNED SPACEFLIGHT
UNMANNED
  SPACEFLIGHT
BRITISH STEAM
  LOCOMOTIVES

The Arts, etc.

ARCHITECTURE
CATHEDRALS
CHURCHES
HERALDRY
FLAGS
PAINTING
MODERN ART
SCULPTURE
FURNITURE
MUSIC
POSTAGE STAMPS
POTTERY AND
  PORCELAIN
BRITISH AWARDS
  & MEDALS
ANCIENT & ROMAN
  BRITAIN
EUROPEAN COSTUME
SEWING

Sport

ASSOCIATION FOOTBALL
CRICKET
GOLF
MOTOR SPORT

Cities

LONDON

The Observer's Book of

EUROPEAN
COSTUME

GEOFFREY SQUIRE

AND

PAULINE BAYNES

FREDERICK WARNE & CO LTD

FREDERICK WARNE & CO INC

LONDON : NEW YORK

© Frederick Warne & Co Ltd
London, England
1975

Dedication

To those dear friends who have helped
during a difficult time

LIBRARY OF CONGRESS CATALOG
CARD NO 74-80613

ISBN 0 7232 1521 9

Printed and bound in Great Britain by
Morrison & Gibb Ltd, London and Edinburgh
129.1174

Contents

Acknowledgements

Dress is a visual subject yet even books on costume are apt to begin with a text for which appropriate illustrations are later chosen. This one began the opposite way round. Without the illustrations it would not have existed at all, and the text owes its inspiration to the work of a learned and gifted artist on whose charming and scrupulously accurate drawings it is a commentary, intended to augment rather than to describe what she had already made so clear. My most grateful thanks, then, are due firstly to Pauline Baynes, the most perceptive, intuitively sympathetic and incisive of collaborators anyone could wish to have. Then to my colleagues and companions Elizabeth Murdoch, who typed most of the manuscript, and Mrs Jane Gardiner, who cheerfully undertook many dull tasks and carried so many very heavy parcels to and from Bedford Square. Thanks to my brother (Father Aelred Squire) who approved the section of this work in which he has particular knowledge, and who also, during a holiday, typed part of the text. Thanks too to my friend Ronald Parkinson, whose tact and consideration at all times equals his ability and exactitude (not for the first time) as a proof-reader. Also I am indebted to Mr David Bisacre and Mrs Ruth Day of Messrs Frederick Warne who have, apparently, the patience of angels – and last but not least to Mr Charles Gibbs-Smith who first so kindly recommended that I should undertake what has been a happy task.

Introduction

'The glass of fashion and the mould of form,
The observed of all observers . . .'
Hamlet Act III, sc. i

Europeans have completely changed the type, structure, shape and style of their clothing many times over the centuries. In no other area of the world has there occurred any comparable phenomenon in the field of dress. Continual and radical change was unique to Europe until, in the 17th century, European settlers established similar principles in their colonies on the American continent. But the alterations, however radical in the long run, have seldom been *suddenly* contradictory. They have, in general, been accomplished through a logical evolution. One type, structure, shape or style has been developed very gradually from another. Occasionally exotic types or details have been borrowed for the sake of variety from the more static societies of the Near or Far East, or from Africa, but these have always been totally adapted to European requirements. In fact, such borrowings have occurred only when developments in European dress were already displaying similar tendencies, so that the exotic examples were received sympathetically. Today European dress has been universally accepted as the standard, and its long tradition of dynamic variability has helped to create a world-wide expectation for frequent alluring innovations. The fashionable dress of Europe, starting as the product of many different crafts, became eventually an exclusive art and then also a popular industry. Now

7

an eager public, at every social level, awaits the biannual appearance of 'the very latest thing', which modern methods of communication can rapidly convey to all classes in all countries from the very moment of its first presentation.

At the same time certain unprovable assumptions concerning costume and its history have been widely accepted to exercise an almost unconscious influence on current attitudes to dress. One tenaciously held idea is that the first function of clothing must have been to provide protection for the vulnerable human body against extremes of climate, and the reasonable supposition follows that it should always be suitably adjustable between light-weight and heavy according to seasonal or climatic conditions. Another is that dress was primarily intended to hide the private parts of the body from public exposure, and that it is consequently an essential guardian of decency. Somewhat contradictory theories suggest that its principal use was provocative. By partial revelation, or suggestive signs, sexual attractiveness could be enhanced and interest encouraged. It has also been very credibly argued that clothes constitute 'status symbols'. If they *are* intended to demonstrate the wearer's hierarchical, regal, noble or professional position or his pecuniary prestige, they must, it is felt, inevitably impart respectability, as well as prove how much money he can afford to waste on unnecessary extravagances. Clothes, it is claimed, should make us *feel* comfortable while helping us to *appear* decent, desirable, respectable and enviable to others. While clearly there is much truth in this, the fact that the whole appearance of European men and women has been so constantly and completely altered by their clothing (much of it of a restrictive, even a deforming kind) suggests that their conception of decency, attractiveness, respectability and even of physical comfort must have been equally mutable. Alternatively, there must be some other yet stronger motivation, which could counteract or over-rule the more obvious and sensible requirements of dress.

Changes in fashionable dress have been ascribed to many and various causes. The rise and fall of reigning houses or of empires; political and matrimonial alliances; wars and revolutions; religious fanaticism and crusading; dramatic developments in agriculture; trade, economics, science, technology, industry and suffrage; mechanical inventions; exploration and discovery – all have been suggested as contributing factors, together with continual competitive rivalry between some traditional nobility or aristocracy and an upstart plutocracy. It has also been supposed that fashions were invariably dictated by monarchs, or the influentially rich and famous, whose personal taste and public position made their ideas seem irresistible – by people such as Catherine de Medici, Louis XIV, Madame de Pompadour, George Brummel or Lily Langtry – or by popular figures, whose eccentric or provocative behaviour caught the general imagination – such as 'Robin Hood', Walter Raleigh, Peg Woffington, the Duke of Wellington, Jean Harlow or the Beatles. Again it has been said, more recently, that designers who chose dress as a medium for their individual artistic expression – men like Worth, Poiret, Dior or Ossie Clark – have frequently forced women to wear garments of outrageous ugliness or impracticability which they would not have tolerated uncoerced. There is some evidence to support the truth of each of these arguments; even enough perhaps to suggest that such considerations can affect the clothes men wear or the appearance they wish to make. And yet, if we ask ourselves again why it is that these things alone should have prompted an apparently uncontrollable and remarkably widespread desire for only certain types, forms and styles *and for no others* at any precise moment of the past it is often difficult to find a credible answer. Items which became 'the fashion' cannot in fact be at all satisfactorily reconciled with all, or indeed any, of the more obvious influences. Indeed, on the contrary, when looking back through the recorded clothing from the past we can see at times dresses accepted as 'the very latest thing' which, although clearly far too thick and heavy for even the coldest winter, have been worn in the height of hot summer. At others, garments scanty enough only for the warmest climate have appeared fashionable in the depth of winter. There have been dresses exposing as much as they concealed, and others exaggerated to the point of caricature to draw attention to the private parts they covered. We can find clothes of inexpensive fabric favoured as 'the very latest thing' only when showing every sign of heavy wear, and functional working gear being welcomed in smart and most exclusive drawing-rooms. Many garments appear to have been constructed expressly to make the human body look as disproportionate, ugly and unattractive as possible, while others have surrounded their owners with seemingly insurmountable hazards and inconveniences, and with only very slight adaptations have formed the dress of working people. Then there have been many daringly dress-conscious individuals of the highest degree or of great prominence or popularity who have yet left no mark of their personal preferences upon the styles of their contemporaries. And many world-renowned designers have seen their favourite effects rejected by an uncomprehendingly hostile public.

It is only when we consider particular developments in European dress in their widest context and in relationship to all the concurrent developments in architecture, painting, sculpture, decoration, literature, music, drama, philosophy, religion, economy, social structure, manners and morals, thought and belief, that we can begin to approach any possible explanation for some of the strange costumes which have been quite happily worn at one time or another. It is only when we accept that *style in dress* is an essential part of a complete *style of life* that we can begin fully to appreciate the significance of the extraordinary structures men have sometimes felt it essential to impose upon the human form – structures that are neither the result of entirely practical nor totally whimsical inclinations. The motives prompting particular changes in the style of dress have been as different as the distinctive shapes themselves. Dress presents a record of Man's aspiration towards an eternally illusive ideal; his attempts to give physical form to mental concepts. Resulting from a potent mixture of attitudes often unrecognized until later, the clothes of every period have themselves provided a really potent force helping to change many existing points of view. Because dress has been readily enjoyed by the frivolous, and has generally been discussed in detail only by the superficial; because it is essentially ephemeral, rapidly losing any immediate significance, and is easily spoiled, soiled, worn-out or destroyed, it has generally been considered of small importance in the history of Man. It has been studied mainly as a curiosity, or to illustrate and fill out historical 'background', in spite of the fact that it formed an important factor in the foreground of its day. In fact the transitory nature of clothing has made it an ideal medium for experiment. The comparative ease with which its principles and appearances can be totally changed has allowed it to become an intimate and subtle indicator of developments in European thought. From such a view it will be treated in this book.

On fairly reliable evidence it is safe to assume that the adornment of the body (firstly with *objet-trouvé*, animal, vegetable, or mineral, followed rapidly by the addition of manufactured articles and accessories of either a functional or decorative kind) preceded the invention of clothing. Clothing throughout the world, wherever or whenever it appears, can be divided into two basic types – *draped* and *shaped*. Contrary to logical expectation *shaped* clothing appears to have been the more primitive of the two. Constructed from the skins of animals which were already shaped by Nature, little imagination was required for their adaptation to the not too dissimilar form of Man. *Draped* clothing became possible only for settled societies with time to invent and perfect the complex rhythmic techniques of spinning, plaiting, knotting, knitting and weaving, and the construction of looms. Some authorities have suggested that *fitted* clothing made from animal hides was the natural product of nomadic hunting peoples living in cold climates, while *draped* clothing, composed from pieces of textile woven from animal or vegetable threads, first appeared in warmer areas with settled populations dependent on agriculture and stock-breeding. Theoretically distinctions have been made between 'arctic' and 'tropical' types of dress. Yet various combinations of both shaped *and* draped items seem to have been general to most early cultures regardless of climatic conditions. While it is true that some examples of very early clothing found in Europe and dating from about 1400 B.C. were made from woven textiles and showed ingenious attempts to imitate the texture and shape of the animal skins which presumably preceded them, it is notable that equal ingenuity was used, at the same time, to construct other garments shaped approximately to the body but without wasting any of the laboriously produced fabric. The first specifically European garments – that is to say garments appearing throughout Europe, as opposed to those confined only to particular tribes or localities – were based upon the generally *draped* types which characterized the Mediterranean civilizations of Greece and Rome evolving between 1200 and 200 B.C. Even there *some* shaping had been introduced due to contacts with, and influences from, the Near East, where shaping of an extreme simplicity had been general to even earlier civilizations. With the vast expansion of the Roman Empire from the 1st century A.D., *barbaric* elements from northern Europe in addition to the refinements from the east continued the infiltration of *shaped* items of dress into general acceptance. But such shaping was always geometrical and all seams were straight. These *shaped* clothes consequently did not *fit*. They were schematic, merely approximating to the very generalized form of a human body standing upright with legs together and arms extended at right angles to the trunk, resembling the letter T. It was not until after the 12th century A.D. that the most important single distinguishing feature of European dress began to emerge, with the introduction of curved seaming, the use of which rapidly increased in complexity. This practice eventually allowed clothing to be fitted very closely to the underlying form of the body – so changing its type as well as its style. But it also involved considerable wastage of woven fabric. The cutting of textiles into shaped sections, which were then joined together again by needlework to form a garment, had never been unique to Europe. But, like the primitive tribes of the Teutonic north and the civilized citizens of the Mediterranean south, all other non-European races throughout the world retained, and continued to retain until modern times, a firm respect for the art of the weaver. Only in Europe was this respect so completely sacrificed to the point where the art of the cutter took precedence. Although to produce even the simplest *shaped* garment, fabric has of necessity to be cut into pieces, this had always been most carefully planned so that every piece was of use. This was possible so long as *straight* seaming and *approximate* 'fit' was the rule (as it still is in the traditional dress of the Near and Far East) and so long as all the sections were based upon the rectangular form imposed by the loom. Then the art of the weaver remained dominant in dress. The quality of fabric and the design of its interwoven pattern were the first aesthetic considerations and the indicators of social standing. But once the sections of a garment were shaped to follow the curving form of the body and its limbs, then the pieces cut away between the variously shaped sections were useless. Some considerable part of the precious woven stuff had become scrap. Soon it was the art of cutting rather than the art of weaving which became the main focus for admiration and praise. The work of the couturier and the tailor dominated. 'Line' superseded fabric as the first sign of artistic refinement and pecuniary power. The body itself began to be dominated by its dress, being often altered out of all human recognition by the abstract shapes imposed upon it by cutting and construction. But these fashionable abstractions were the outward revelation of an inner questing spirit which was working to create the environment in which the men and women of Europe were to live. It is the relationship between the developments in thought and shape which this book will try to explain.

In the study of costume certain distinctions must be made between fashionable dress, customary dress, practical dress and *haute-couture*.

The term *fashionable dress* refers to those styles which, originating among an élite minority at a court, or some equivalent social focus of popular attention, win wide approval and by rapid emulation become general practice for the majority within a short time.

Customary dress has its origins in particular items of once-fashionable dress, which are retained in a conventionalized or fossilized form for ceremonial, ritualistic or other specific purposes long after their general use has been discontinued. These then provide marks of distinction to separate the chosen from the many, and to eliminate as far as possible the effects of individual personality – as, for example, the vestments of a priest, or the robes and wig of a judge.

Practical dress consists of garments made to fulfil a precise utilitarian purpose, for which their use is usually reserved. Though initially designed to be protective, hard-wearing, or to allow ease of movement in the performance of a particular task, such clothing has frequently been influential upon more purely decorative fashionable dress, and, on occasion, has been adopted *as* fashionable dress. The 18th century sailor's wide trousers and bob-tailed jacket provided inspiration for the first liberating fashionable clothes for small boys. The coachman's many-caped overcoat was speedily adopted for smart wear as long-distance travel became frequent. Cowboys' 'jeans' proved an ideal uniform for equality-conscious youth after the Second World War. Workmen's dungarees have recently been smartly re-interpreted in velveteen by an affluent society whose influential members wished to emphasize their proletarian origins without denying their preference for luxury.

Haute-couture (high-fashion or fine-cut[1]) is a term limited to the designs of an artist who uses the dress of other people as a medium for his personal expression. Conceived for an idealized, non-existent figure rather than for a particular living individual, such designs *may* become fashionable after adaptation by a manufacturer, or they may have only a very limited effect, remaining single works of art displayed in an exclusive show-room to attract the discerning collector, and appearing only within the confines of a wealthy and élite coterie. They are more indicative of the personal taste of the designer and his patron than of the style of an age – although they will inevitably reflect some

---

[1] The literal translation of *couturer* is 'to seam', but as the most important contribution of the modern *couturier* has been in the subtle shaping and placing of seams resulting from *cutting* rather than in the quality of stitching, I have preferred to associate the term with cut. G.S.

aspects of that style. *Haute-couture* is a very specialized branch of fashionable dress unknown before 1860 and diminishing in importance after 1960.

It is with *fashionable dress* as defined in the first section above that this book is principally concerned, although from the other definitions it must be apparent that both customary and practical dress will be discussed where exact distinctions are impossible since contrary motivations are at work – as is usual in the dress of the middle and working classes. It is worth noting, however, that at any time the majority has made *some* attempt to approximate to the currently fashionable ideal. By following the main lines of development in this essentially civil and secular art, and by studying its changes in conjunction with contemporary aesthetic and social transformations, the important part played by clothing in the formation and propagation of European culture is revealed.

Editorial Note

Words in **bold type** indicate the first important appearance in the book of a specific dress term, and if not fully explained in the text will be found in the Glossary and Explanatory Notes section on p. 150.

Roman (1st–3rd centuries)

The first specifically European costume was that of the Romans. By A.D. 138 their empire extended from north Britain to the Sahara; from the Euphrates to the west coast of Spain. Over this vast area, united under the *Pax Romana*, Latin culture flourished among many differing races. Indigenous customs and clothing yielded to Roman adaptations of a Greek legacy. The Latins had emulated native Greek logic, reason, order and moderation, and a speculative inquiry into the nature of Man which illuminated philosophy, art and dress. To this heritage the practical, energetic Romans added their particular interests in law, literature, architecture and engineering. This vital combination laid the foundation for European civilization. Roman dress only slightly modified Greek practice; added volume, and then sumptuousness.

Roman (1st–3rd centuries)

Many Greco-Roman garments were simply rectangles of linen or woollen, wrapped, brooched or tied around the body allowing easy movement. Softly draping textiles made their own aesthetically pleasing effects. Little was done to the material to limit its use to clothing, or its wear to one sex or an individual figure. The arrangement of this temporary, adaptable type of dress depended upon the skill of the wearer. Its several insecurely fixed layers required continual readjustment. Form was given by the body, over which this clothing hung, fluid, unrestricting, and responding harmoniously to every movement. Physical freedom was valued, and humans, naked and unashamed (as they appeared daily at the public baths) provided the principal subject for sculpture and painting.

Roman (1st–3rd centuries)

One garment – the **tunica** – was given *permanent* structure. An oblong length of fabric, folded and partially stitched together on each side, left openings for head and arms. Tubular sleeves were frequently added, at right angles. But in the construction of this simple robe no precious fabric was wasted. The tunica, loose, unparticularized, egalitarian, could be worn by both sexes and all sizes. A girdle was placed high by women to hold their full-length garments. The (generally shorter) clothes of men were belted low. Such detail only, together with hair-styles and jewellery, marked sexual and individual differences. Male hair was cut short. Women dressed long tresses close to the head in elaborate plaits, coils and curls.

Roman (1st–3rd centuries)

The most distinctively Roman garment was the **toga**.
An enormous outer wrap, it was unusual in being
(wastefully) *cut* into shape (the segment of a circle) and
in its exclusive reservation to formal dress for male
citizens. Originally of moderate size, it expanded by
the 1st century B.C. to measure over 18ft (5m), by 7ft
(2m) deep at the centre, and was draped in a highly
complicated manner. For travel or work smaller
rectangular or semi-circular cloaks were simply
brooched on one shoulder. Women wore the **palla**,
a long rectangle not as voluminous as the toga. Sandals
and open-fronted boots left width for the natural
expansion of the toes, and were common to both sexes.
Clothes complemented the body; added dignity; but
were unassertive.

Early Christian (3rd–5th centuries) and

From the 1st century A.D. the original Mediterranean simplicity of dress began to change as affluence and disparate influences from distant parts of the empire took effect. Silk, imported from the Orient, increased sumptuousness and luxury. During the 2nd century the **dalmatic** was adopted. This loose eastern over-garment with wide sleeves was frequently decorated with coloured bands (**clavi**) and often fringed. Christianity (also Near-Eastern in origin) gained converts, and was officially accepted in A.D. 392. The daily wear of Roman Christians provided the basis for eucharistic vestments. Such garments included the **paenula**. This single-seamed, funnel-shaped outer cape, much worn by ordinary men and women, was to evolve into the **chasuble**. In oriental fashion, women's heads were covered by richly patterned turbans and veils.

Byzantine (5th–12th centuries)

During the years of uncertainty barbarian influences from the north mixed with sophisticated influences from the east and, together with the growing appeal of Christianity, began to change peoples' outlook and the character of their dress. While formal clothes became more exotic, impressive and decorative, the new religion proclaimed the subordination of the physical to the spirit. Whenever possible bodies now remained covered. Shape (particularly the shape of Woman who had prompted Man's fall from Grace) was permanently obscured under layers of still unfitted but more securely constructed clothing. Sleeves of under-tunics were made long and close. Male legs, left free for action by short tunics, were closely covered by narrow thongings, hose or breeches, all borrowed from northern barbarians.

Byzantine (5th–12th centuries)

The empire was breaking up: attacked from without by oriental rivals and barbaric tribes, it was divided against itself within. By the 6th century the main power remained with the emperor at Byzantium in the east, while the west was split into Lombard, Frankish, Gothic and Saxon kingdoms. Peace and unity had gone, leaving only a memory in fossilizing Roman dress. In the east, Byzantine ceremonial wear remained unchanged for five hundred years. There, richness was all. Silks, brocaded (*see* Glossary) or embroidered in multi-coloured patterns and gold, were decorated with applied goldsmithery and gems until the fabric hung heavy, stiff and angular. In art the human figure lost all naturalism, becoming schematic, the fullness of folds reduced to a decorative linear pattern.

Byzantine (5th–12th centuries)

The toga, conventionally folded to seem only a long, stiffly decorated and pleated band, was gradually superseded by the **pallium** (the name used for the rectangular wrap when worn by men); or a semi-circular cloak fastened on the right shoulder was decorated for formal wear with the **tablion** (a large patch of rich embroidery). Both palla and pallium were folded and bound firmly round the body in a spiral; or wrapped tightly about the waist and draped over the left side. A narrow variant of the pallium had a hole for the head, the front section hanging straight to the feet, the back brought forward under one arm and thrown across the other like a scarf. Regal heads wore jewelled tiaras.

Romanesque (10th–12th centuries)

Even in the chaotic west the fading spirit of the empire never totally disappeared. It hovered like a dream during four hundred years of turmoil, invasions, subjugation and revolt. Its legacy of one language and one style of dress had permeated all Europe to preserve its memory and serve as recurring inspiration to the idealistic. From the 5th to the 11th centuries a new social and cultural pattern was slowly forged. Based insecurely upon Roman heritage, it had acquired by the 9th century a distinctive character from a complex intermingling of different races and traditions. Paganism had retreated before Christian missionary zeal, leaving the power of the Church as a factor to dominate even monarchy. Clothing changed little in principle, though away from direct Byzantine control it was never so stylized or richly decorated.

Romanesque (10th–12th centuries)

Something of original softness and simplicity blended with more robust and eccentric barbarian derivations. Toga and pallium were everywhere discarded for utilitarian rectangular or semi-circular **mantles**, fastened on one shoulder to leave the sword-arm free. The geometric T-shaped tunic had long been modified by inserting triangular **gores** into each side below the waist to give extra fullness at the skirt hem. Barbarian fashions for leg-bandages, trousers, beards and longer hair for men became established practice. Women's bodies were muffled in shapeless floor-length **gowns** and closed square- or extinguisher-shaped mantles. Their 'crowning glory' now 'a snare of the devil' disappeared completely under scarves and linen veils.

Romanesque (10th–12th centuries)

The uncertainties of life had produced necessary organizations for people seeking support and re-assurance. Communities of celibate ascetics devoted entirely to religious observances were eventually institutionalized as monasteries. There the ideal of personal poverty led to the use of common possessions for ambitious programmes of building centred on a majestic house of God. A secular counterpart was provided by groups of small holders who offered services and produce in return for military protection by a local overlord, whose castle and army of retainers offered hope of common safety. Learning and the arts were preserved and encouraged mainly by the Church, in the enrichment of which they were almost exclusively employed. In dress, it was still in details, not basic forms, that sexual differences were maintained.

Romanesque (10th–12th centuries)

The most formative influences were religion and militarism – neither encouraging whimsical innovation, but both tending to emphasize order in a hierarchy. Monarchs and their courts still emulated Byzantine pomp, but achieved often only a ruder, artless barbaric splendour. From the 11th century newer, exotic elements appeared, due to contacts with the expanded power of Islam. Arabian possessions in North Africa, Spain and southern France, and the Arab-orientated Norman 'Kingdom of the Two Sicilies' provided superb silks, rich craft products rivalling those of the eastern empire, and introduced new fashions for long, hanging sleeves, and horizontal bands of pattern to add to the sumptuous embroidery at necks, hems and biceps.

Early Gothic (12th–14th centuries)

Six crusades between 1095 and 1228 added oriental plunder to trade goods and increased the effects of Islamic influence in dress, decoration and architectural detail. As a new sophisticated assurance reappeared, feudalism formalized into the romantic concept of chivalry. In southern France and Germany troubadours and minnesingers celebrated this amalgamation of barbarian-secular and Christian-religious ideology which provided women with an important civilizing role as the objects of courtly love. Enlightened minds also looked back admiringly to the classical past, and bodies began to emerge from heavy wrappings. Attempts were made to mould garments closely to the torso using first the basic tunic form, which, by being laced on each side from armpit to hip, was *dragged* to fit.

Early Gothic (12th-14th centuries)

Laces produced complex wrinkling which artists, often still working in Celtic or barbaric traditions, interpreted as elaborate linear pattern. Meanwhile military necessity had suggested an insulating garment to be worn beneath the weight of armour, and practicality required that this should fit closely. A padded tunic with curving seams at centre front and back as well as beneath each arm (later called the **doublet**) hinted at a new possibility eventually to affect the appearance of both men and women. Married women continued eastern practice in covering the head to obscure the hair. Unmarried girls exploited this attractive asset by plaiting it into **casings**, which appeared to extend its length, or left it hanging free. A new inventiveness was seen in **surcoats**, ingeniously combining the principles of tunic and mantle in one garment.

Early Gothic (12th–14th centuries)

But still the main principles of dress were *shared* by men and women. Whether loose, in the classical tradition, or approximately fitted, in the new manner, skirted tunics were cut without a waist seam. Some male garments had full-length skirts, but these were usually left open on the sides, or at front and back, to allow for ease in riding. Tunics were layered, one over another, the outer layer, or surcoat, being frequently shorter at hem and sleeves to display the narrower under-tunic. These surcoats and also mantles were generally lined with fur, which was arranged in neat repeating patterns by using the backs and bellies of the squirrel, or pelts of different colours.

Early Gothic (12th–14th centuries)

Hooded capes of various lengths, descended from the Roman paenula, continued their utilitarian use, while male heads were additionally covered by close-fitting **coifs** tied under the chin, or by small beret-like hats. Only men wore loose linen drawers or **braies** reaching to below the knee, and supported by a cord, channelled through the waist. Over these were drawn hose, of woven fabric cut on the bias-grain to give some elasticity. From a point on the thigh the hose were tied to the cord which held the braies. Female hose rose only to just above the knee where they were gartered. Shoes were identical for both sexes. Fitted, but softly flexible, they followed the natural lines of the foot, tending to an extended point beyond the large toe.

Early Gothic (12th–14th centuries)

During the 'Age of Faith' the majority of people, tied to the land whether as serfs or freemen, worked from sun-up to sun-down, spring, summer, autumn and winter. This regular, natural routine had its counterpart in the offices of the Church which marked the climactic moments of the year by feast-days and festivals (pagan celebrations, Christianized as 'holy-days', being interspersed among more authentically religious commemorations). Huge cathedrals rising between the 10th and 15th centuries provided the focus for devotion as well as spectacular terrestrial prospects of the celestial City of God. These creations of masons and craftsmen were made possible by unstinted offerings from lord and peasant, and within their walls all men were equal in the eyes of God.

Early Gothic (12th–14th centuries)

In 1144 the abbey-church of Saint Denis outside Paris crystallized changes in architecture from the bulky Romanesque forms (which had emphasized simple mass and weight, using barrel vaults, round arches and thick piers, all derived from Roman precedent) into the lighter Gothic style (which emphasized springing height, by slender columns and pointed arches forming a delicate grid-like framework, supported by flying buttresses and filled with coloured glass, its flaming crocketed skyline dissolving upwards into air). From the 12th century, too, the busy new towns which had clustered spontaneously around the cathedrals grew in size and importance. Merchants, traders and craftsmen began to form an intermediate urban group between the rural nobility and peasants.

Early Gothic (12th–14th centuries)

Clothes at all social levels continued similar in form. The simplest of cut and construction were normal tailoring practice. But, naturally, individuals at every level adapted the simple forms to their particular requirements. Men, working in the fields, opened the split skirts of their short tunics and tucked the front corners into their belts behind, revealing ill-fitting hose and a glimpse of braies. Or, removing homespun tunic and hose, tied up the long legs of their loose drawers to the waist-cord, and went barefoot. A less energetic overseer might wear a short, sleeveless surcoat; a conical straw hat; and roll down his hose below the calf. Women, hair securely braided and almost hidden by linen cauls, hoods or wrapped scarves, covered

Early Gothic (12th–14th centuries)

practical, ankle-length skirts with large aprons, and often wore protective, gauntleted gloves – similar to, but not so fine as, those worn by the lord-of-the-manor as a guard against the claws of his hawk. The prosperous city merchant wore his tunic of solid cloth comfortably loose; long enough for dignity, but short enough for bustling about the town. On cold days a surcoat with **fitchets** (pocket-slits) allowed him to keep his hands warm or to reach his purse, safely belted underneath. His wife, respectably gowned and mantled, wrapped neck and chin in a clean linen **wimple** and covered her head with a neatly pressed and folded veil.

Early Gothic (12th–14th centuries)

One variant of the surcoat, worn by all classes from the mid-13th century, was the **garnache**. Long or short, it was cut very wide at the shoulder, forming cape-like sleeves falling to about elbow level. It frequently had tongue-shaped lapels at the neck, and was worn loose or belted. Other surcoats, often worn by women, were without sleeves, the arm openings cut away deeply towards the waist. Among the new, bi-sexual hat shapes of the 14th century was one with a wide brim, partly turned up to leave the remainder in a projecting peak. Worn with the peak forward it shaded eyes from the sun; with the peak backwards it protected the nape. Hats were placed over or under hoods according to whim.

Early Gothic (12th–14th centuries)

The hood, its shoulder-cape varying from a few inches beyond the throat to as deep as elbow level, began to have an extra extension – the **liripipe** – attached to its point. When worn by women (over the head veil) the hood was usually left unstitched below the chin, hanging open to reveal the wimple. This neck-cloth covered the throat to the chin and was pinned up to the netted coils of hair at each side. From about 1320 (as Gothic style in all the arts tended increasingly to elegant elongation, refined attenuation, and the use of swaying ogival curves) the clothes, first of men, and a little later of women, were increasingly cut with curving seams to an ever closer fit.

International Gothic (Late 14th–15th centuries)

Worn above a close, military **arming-doublet**, the new **cote-hardie** emphasized slender lines. Made to fit smoothly over the torso as far as the hips, it then flared gently into a fuller skirt. Its sleeves, closely cut, finished generally at the elbow in a pendant flap, displaying the even closer doublet sleeve on the forearm, laced or buttoned from elbow to wrist. Belts worn about the hips, *not* at the waist, stressed length. The capes of hoods were, fashionably, **dagged** (cut into tongue or leaf-shaped tabs). By 1350 smart young women were wearing their own adaptation of the masculine cote-hardie; its neck cut wide rather than low; its skirt spreading softly from the hip to fall in deep folds which rested on the floor.

International Gothic (Late 14th–15th centuries)

Conservative people continued to wear unfitted clothes; conservative women continued to cover necks with wimples and heads with veils. But fashionable girls and ladies at the courts displayed their hair again, elaborately plaited and coiled over each ear. Male hair, cut to just below the ear, was dressed in artfully arranged curls. A great fashion of the 13th and 14th centuries was **parti-colouring**. Military in origin it had been an aid to identification on the battlefield; a knight's retainers dressing in his colours. While clothes were primarily a proclamation of social standing, parti-colouring in civilian life retained much heraldic significance, but increasingly added capricious gaiety to the still simple forms of fashion.

International Gothic (Late 14th–15th centuries)

Towards the end of the 14th century much greater variety was to be found in dress. Citizens, their wealth accumulating from trading and banking, made splendid town-houses centres for display, to compete with, and stimulate, even more refined splendours at courts. The old technique of layered garments achieved new sophistication in the **sideless-surcoat**. Very subtle cutting was required for this exclusively feminine dress, in which the body part was reduced to a shoulder-band and pendant central panel from which the skirt was suspended below the hip-line. Immense concave side openings revealed the form-fitting cotehardie beneath. Sometimes, too, the seams of the skirt were almost completely unstitched for greater effect.

International Gothic (Late 14th–15th centuries)

The vestigial upper part of the sideless-surcoat was often covered entirely in fur, its front section (the **plackard**) decorated with jewelled bosses which held the garment in place by buttoning through from, or hooking on to, the underdress. Several veils of fine, stiffened linen gauze with closely goffered or ruched edges, forming a frilly arch round the face, were fashionable between 1350 and 1420. After sixty years of form-fitting variants on the cote-hardie, men reacted by covering the doublet with voluminous **houppelandes**. These Hispano-Arabian robes spread out from the shoulder to an enormous circumference, the fullness held in place by a rich belt. For additional splendour a mantle was sometimes placed over all.

International Gothic (Late 14th–15th centuries)
During the course of the 14th century there had appeared a gradual secularization in all the arts; evident even in work commissioned for or by the Church. Precious, delicate, decorative and highly sophisticated, emphasis was laid on elegance and fantasy, and this final flamboyant development of the Gothic permeated from its centre in the courts of France and Burgundy to affect England, Italy, Germany and Bohemia. A delight in imaginative inventiveness was accompanied by a new interest in natural detail, which was used for decorative ends. In dress, though country people, city workers, craftsmen and merchants continued to wear the simple, now traditional, forms still unadapted to a new outlook, the courts led an unprecedented indulgence in variety, extravagance and whimsical exaggeration.

International Gothic (Late 14th–15th centuries)

From about 1350 the fashionable doublet and cote-hardie began gradually to be shortened year by year. This necessitated the complementary lengthening of the hose. The function of supporting these stockings (still woven, bias-cut, and tailored) was transferred from the cord of the braies to the skirts of the doublet. The tops of the hose were tied by several **points** (short laces with metal tags) through eyelet-holes worked into the doublet's lower edge. When dressed the wearer was literally 'trussed-up'. The gap at fork and seat (through which the now much-reduced, brief linen drawers appeared) was hidden on most occasions by the slightly longer skirt of the cote-hardie, often made with a high collar and full sleeves by 1380.

International Gothic (15th century)

The doublet had also increased in rigidity, its upper part fully and roundly padded out, its skirt, below the waist, laced as tightly as a corset. This firm foundation, exaggerating masculine characteristics of deep chest and narrow hips, gave form to the newly fashionable houppelande, which was worn over it from 1380. This full gown, variable in length (as short as the thigh, or sweeping on to the floor), had immense funnel-shaped, or full bagpipe sleeves, a high collar, a fur lining, and was often dagged. Belted at hip level it emphasized the bulk of the torso. By 1400 women followed masculine example and adopted the houppelande. Identical in cut and all other detail, a slightly different appearance was given only by belting it immediately beneath the breasts and leaving it unfastened at the

neck, opening in a deep V down to the high waist. The form-fitting female cote-hardie and sideless-surcoat were generally relegated to ceremonial wear after 1400. A riot of fantasy in headgear was initiated by men. The caped hood, no longer indispensable with the advent of high collars, was put on with the head in the face-opening, leaving the elaborately dagged and decorated cape to hang on one side, while the scarf-like liripipe was draped over shoulders and chest; or both were wound together into a temporary turban. This was later 'made-up' into a more permanent formal hat (the **chaperon**) by adding a thickly padded cylindrical brim.

International Gothic (15th century)

The chaperon was quickly adapted to feminine use by increasing the size of the padded roll, and bending it into a heart-shape to fit over the two plaited knobs into which the hair was dressed at the temples. Alternatively these horns of hair (usually cased in silk nets or openwork metal **templers**) were surmounted by the traditional linen or gauze veil, now held away from the head on wire supports. Until about 1435 female headgear emphasized width; after that, height. Other hats for men and women were mostly variations on the padded roll, the turban and the bag. Exclusively masculine were those of beaver or finely plaited, lacquered straw with balloon-shaped crowns and drooping brims. The most fashionable masculine hair-style during the first half of the 15th century was the

bowl-crop. For this the nape and side hair was shaved, leaving a thick, short pad, like a skull-cap, on the crown.

The most favoured weaving thread was now silk. Produced throughout Italy and Spain, types included plain and figured velvets, satins, damasks and brocades; or combinations of these weaves, incorporating much gold thread. Designs continued mainly oriental in derivation. Small-patterned silks from 14th century Lucca, showing strong Chinese influence, were superseded in the 15th century by those from Florence, Venice and Genoa, in which much larger formal patterns were inspired by Ottoman Turkish originals. Florence and Flanders continued to weave English wool into fine plain cloth.

49

International Gothic (15th century)

Workers, servants and country folk wore coarser homespun cloth of wool and linen. Their general appearance was not so very different from that of their Romanized ancestors of a thousand years before, their garments being generally cut for ease. The poorer hose of energetic field-hands or city craftsmen were seldom fitted with precision, and although theoretically trussed to the lined (but unpadded) doublet they were rarely fastened, since the strutting-restricted deportment imposed by the fashionable ideal would have been somewhat of an obstacle in a working life. Only in details like hats, pouches, purses and occasionally dagged hems was there much evidence of changing style in the clothing worn by working men.

International Gothic (15th century)

For all women, high or low, the **kirtle** was the main foundation garment, as the doublet was for men. This *shaped* successor to the almost shapeless tunic laced in front or under each arm. Fashionably hidden under cote-hardie or houppelande, outside the limited circles with pretensions to modishness, it was the *major* garment. Often turned up for convenience, beneath it was revealed the short linen **shift**; a woman's only underwear. The long sleeves of the shift were exposed on the arm, appearing through the very short, narrow sleeve of the kirtle. At smarter social levels separate fore-sleeves of sumptuous fabric were pinned or tied on to those of the kirtle, to show at the opening of more splendid outer gowns. Hoods and head-wraps for daily wear were more utilitarian than fanciful, and aprons protected better gowns.

International Gothic (Mid-15th century)

With the middle years of the 15th century the various trends begun by the fashionable over fifty years before were carried to a climax. The modes originated in north-western Europe appeared with only minor variations in the south and east. Volume everywhere increased and so did weight. Robes lay on the ground in front of the wearer and long trains swept the floor behind. Sleeves too cascaded to the garment's hem. Double- and triple-piled velvets were further decorated by multi-coloured brocading, and plain fabrics were thickly embroidered with silk, gold, pearls and gem-stones. Linings of contrasting colour or design were displayed when the gown was gathered up for walk-ing. Many robes were lined with fur, or at least edged and faced with it in deep bands.

International Gothic (Mid-15th century)

Dagging ran riot; capes and sleeves and veils for head-dresses as well as hems were cut into fluttering scalloped ribbons, and some clothes were trimmed with deep, knotted and spaced fringes. Such dress demanded a slow and stately deportment to set it off, and was especially suited to impressive public ceremonial parades. In Italy, while general practice and appearance conformed to Burgundian dictates, it was noticeable that the high head-dresses of women were formed usually from their own hair, which was not totally concealed as in the north. And men more readily revealed the tight foundation of doublet and hose, seen through the open sides of a decorative **tabard**, or worn with no additional garments above.

International Gothic (Late 15th century)

An artistic expression in decline is characterized by tendencies to over-formalization, needless elaboration and self-caricature. The final waning of the essential spirit of the Middle Ages during the decades of 1460 and 1470 was marked in its centres of origin – France, Burgundy and Flanders – by extravagant romantic court ceremonials in which extreme theatricality in dress played an important part. The male doublet, skin tight and thickly padded, was shortened to the hip-bones. The hose, lengthened yet again to meet it, were joined at the seat, and the gap at the fork concealed under a triangular gusset (the **codpiece**) to form 'tights'. At the tops of the sleeves round hard pads (**mahoitres**), resembling cannon-balls, exaggerated the breadth of the shoulder.

International Gothic (Late 15th century)

These pads widely distended the tubular sleeves of the gown worn over the doublet. This gown, a formalization of the houppelande, had its fullness set into symmetrical flutes, each padded and stitched permanently into position, holding the garment in stiff regularity. High crowns to hats and long points to shoes, together with the towering head-dresses of women, provided a final defiant flourish of the slender spiring Gothic lines, formulated in architecture two hundred years earlier. Steeple-shaped **hennins** were given additional airy height by wired veils of gauze. Deeper necklines marked by broad revers; wider belts; the tightest sleeves; and more slender skirts; all helped towards extreme abstraction in which the natural proportions of the body were dissipated.

International Gothic (Late 15th century)

Only in the daily wear of the vast majority of the working population – peasant, craftsman or servant – was some respect for the natural appearance and mobility of the human body necessarily maintained. But even here sheer practicality could not completely over-rule the style of the age. Doublets were worn, if left unlaced. Hose were used, if rolled down or covered over for extra warmth by leggings tied on with cord; or were protected by knee-pads; and not infrequently they continued to be worn even when out at knee, toe and ankle. Extra protective layers for the body were made large for easy movement; left open at the neck; slit at the sides; and sleeves rolled up. Heads were equipped with both coifs and hats and often hoods as well. In an age when all clothing

International Gothic (Late 15th century)

consisted of 'separates', an assorted collection of garments was piled on or taken off to suit the moment. But the various parts conformed in principle to cut and construction of smarter tailoring practice. And so did the clothing of all children. New-born babies were **swaddled**: bound tightly from neck to feet in wide bands of linen or soft woollen, their arms held close to their sides, their limbs and bodies firmly encouraged to grow straight. As soon as they could stand they were dressed for the most part exactly like their elders. Children were looked on as unformed adults, and their clothes as well as their training, and formal education too if they received any, were all calculated to complete the full development as rapidly as possible.

Renaissance (Late 15th–early 16th centuries)

Just as the medieval world had been created within and from the disintegrating structure of the Roman Empire, so the concept termed Renaissance began to emerge among the meaningless elaborations engendered by the declining Gothic. In Italy the new spirit was evident as early as the 14th century, and clarified there before the middle of the 15th. Gothic style and Gothic thought, native to France and the north, had never flourished well in the former heartland of the old empire, where the spirit of antiquity had remained, enfeebled, but a force. Late in the 15th century all Europe, tired of ideas and ideals which had lost dynamic life and meaning, and feeling the need for change, saw that changes were already under way in the south.

Renaissance (Late 15th–early 16th centuries)

Europe turned again to Italy. Italianate fashions in dress as well as in architecture and the arts provided an answer to the general need for change. Fashionable dress – the most easily transportable of all media – abandoning its ostentatious effects of fantasy and abstraction seemed to move, in its newly found simplicity, towards the unexaggerated clothing of ordinary men and women, in which awareness of the body had never entirely disappeared. The old forms – doublet and hose – kirtle and gown – remained to form the basis from which a new expression would be formed. But human proportion was restored to favour. A renewed equality between all humans was visually expressed.

Renaissance (Late 15th–early 16th centuries)

The softer, less demonstrative lines which appeared in the prosperous Italian city-states during the 1470s were not in essentials very different from those general to Europe. For women, high-waisted gowns opened in a deep V on the chest, to show the square *décolletage* of the kirtle. But usually the gowns were only slightly trained or hemmed just to touch the ground, so that they hung more compactly about the figure to emphasize its simple mass. Heads, no longer surmounted by monstrously ingenious flights of fancy, were covered only by small close caps, or simple **cauls**; the hair, braided, curled or flowing free to make its own effect.

Renaissance (Late 15th–early 16th centuries)

Men left the doublet (now shortened to the natural waist) open on the front showing the soft gathers of a low-necked shirt; their decorated hose called attention to their bodies and legs which they displayed with virile pride. Sleeves, for both men and women, loosely tied into armholes and only partly fastened on the forearm, allowed easy movement, while the shirt sleeves, puffing through the openings, suggested informality. The huge, sweeping, pleated masculine Gothic gowns were reduced in volume, and worn unfastened. Male hair was grown again to fall naturally to shoulder length. Hats were low and neat. Shoes, closely modelled to the foot, gave natural breadth for toes. By 1490 Italian style was European fashion.

Renaissance (Early 16th century)

Although minds may constantly turn back with admiration to some distant past, they seldom completely deny the intervening developments. Admiration for the classical world (naturally most evident in architectural detail and in sculpture) could never quite destroy the taste for the luxurious splendours enjoyed by late medieval Christendom. In dress – even in Italy – imitation of antiquity never exceeded the vague hints suggested by asymmetrically draping the masculine gown about the clearly defined body, securely covered in its modified but surviving Gothic garments. But a new geometric regularity of line and an unassertive suggestion of gracious dignified nobility gave some evidence of the admiration for the *spirit* of antiquity and its logic, reason, moderation and humanity.

Renaissance (Early 16th century)

In north-western Europe indigenous Gothic tendencies were only partially eroded. In dress, surviving elements from the immediate past were less completely adapted to the new ideas with which they mixed. Modest variations of the hood made women's hair invisible. Bell-shaped sleeves were usual; and a conventual appearance only little relieved by fanciful compromises, such as medieval sideless-surcoats split at the front in the Italian manner to show an undergown. Masculine jerkins (descendants of the old cote-hardie or the short houppelande) had full skirts of stitched, formal pleats joined at the waist to simple, Italianate, square-looking bodies. A love of pattern-making was seen in such detail as contrasting linings puffing through the slashed brims of bonnets.

Renaissance (Early 16th century)

The simplicity of form (closely dependent upon the natural proportion of the human frame) which had marked dress while philosophy and art were principally concerned to discover and express the perfectability of Man – the measure of all things: the microcosm made in the image of God – was not to last for long. Having received a most complete realization in Italy, and having had some influence throughout the west, already during the first quarter of the 16th century the geometric effects began to be exaggerated; dignity and nobility to be more theatrically expressed; increasing weight and volume to create a more conscious 'presence'. Sleeves more fully puffed; collars and revers cut more broad and square; close-set pleats increased in number; all added thickness to the figure.

Renaissance (Early 16th century)

Both men and women assumed a new appearance of massive, ponderous splendour. Rich dark fabrics (turned back, or slashed across to show the sumptuousness of fur linings) were decorated with broad bands of dramatically contrasting velvet, or elaborate, gem-set, geometrically patterned embroidery to emphasize breadth. But, while male clothing was suggesting a caricature of powerful muscularity, a new possibility began to be evident in the dress of women. The front of the gown, drawn tightly across the torso by placing straight vertical seams immediately in front of each armpit, compressed the breasts, forcing them upwards to bulge above the square *décolletage*. The bodice, fitted closely at the back, was joined there to a trained skirt set on in deep pleats behind, emphasizing the full curve of the buttocks below the waist.

Renaissance (Early 16th century)

The aggressive solidity of appearance which characterized dress in the 1520s and '30s was seen at its most extreme in the Germanic areas to the north and east. There tremendous breadth, combined with the boldest, most profligate use of **slashing**, gave to masculine clothing a fantastic air of brutality, enhanced by the wearing of many massive chains in rich goldsmith-work. Hose were now divided into two main parts: **nether-stocks** below the knee; **upper-stocks** above. In practice the pieces were still generally stitched together into a single garment. The upper-stocks were cut into ribbons, allowing full linings to burst through in huge blister-like puffs, and the padded-out codpiece was often made as big as an orange. One

Renaissance (Early 16th century)

distinctive feature of Germanic dress, shared by male and female alike, was the very fine pleating of the under-linen, held closely about the throat by high-quality embroidery of simple design but delicate execution. Such superb shirts and shifts were to be retained for centuries as part of folk-dress; as also were the closely cartridge-pleated skirts, and richly worked **stomachers** which showed as a broad band across the breasts of women. In France women covered the hair with a velvet hood, formalized by a stiff, crescent-shaped front border. In England the most characteristic head-dress was an angular 'gable' form of hood developed from the hennin. Teutonic women covered their plaits with deep cauls, sometimes surmounted by broad-brimmed hats decorated with feathers or jewelled pendants, similar to those worn by men.

Renaissance (Early 16th century)

The effects of intensive intellectual activity felt all over Europe in the 15th and 16th centuries (and today covered by the term 'Renaissance') were many and various. A renewed awareness of the individual person was accompanied by an entirely new awareness of the individuality of particular cities, regions and nations. Local idiosyncrasies of dress in Italy, France, Spain and Germany began to be developed and worn with pride to set new fashions elsewhere. Clothes in a foreign mode were the mark of the travelled, the educated, the smart and the snobbish. German fashions gradually surpassed those of Italy in wide popularity as the effects of the Reformation (another instance of the vigorous rethinking of the age) caught the imagination of those for whom declining spirituality

in the Church was undermining faith.

Central Europe seethed with crisis. In 1524 reformed religion was one factor in a peasants' revolt and the demand for communal sharing of property. But however such philosophical or ethical problems might affect the lives of servants or peasants, their appearance still linked them more closely to the fading Gothic past than to the emerging world. Only in minor details (the squarer shape of shoes or hats, the fuller form of a sleeve, a closer cap or caul instead of scarf or veil) was there much evidence of changing visual style. Yet such details did add their note of change to a general picture, identifiable as a period different from all former times.

Mannerism (1550–1570)

The extraordinary fashions of the second half of the 16th century seem explicable only after reference to developments made in painting and architecture during the preceding twenty-five years. Then younger artists had started reaction in two ways against that ideal perfection set by the great Italians of the quattrocento. Either, by conscious over-refinement, they produced effects of the most extreme artificial elegance – or, by reversal, saw great beauty in ugliness. Their style is now termed 'Mannerist', and something of its paradoxical strangeness began to be exploited in fashionable dress from 1540 onwards. The possibilities of perfection and distortion inherent in tailoring were carried to the ultimate after 1560.

Mannerism (1550–1570)

The male doublet was made as stiff, smooth, tight and wasp-waisted as a corset. The upper-stocks or **trunk-hose** began to swell with padding into monstrous pumpkin-shaped hips. The exaggeratedly 'feminine' silhouette was counterbalanced by a new vogue for beards and short hair, and the natural appearance of the male leg below the thigh – now displayed in separate **stockings** of knitted silk. The female bodice, constructed still by a male tailor – and resembling closely the masculine doublet – flattened the breasts, and masculine hats covered female heads. Below the waist, a **farthingale**, shaped by graduated hoops of cane, distended skirts into smoothly regular bells, concealing the form and motion of the lower limbs.

Mannerism (1570s–1580s)

The narrow frill, into which the fullness of the shirt and shift had been gathered at the neck, became a focus for attention. Appearing above the immensely high cylindrical collar of the doublet in the 1570s, it gradually grew in size to reach a maximum during the 1580s. This **ruff** or **band** had then to be constructed as a separate item. Stiffly starched; 'under-propped' by frames of wire or collars of card (**under-proppers**); edged with fine spiky lace from Italy or Flanders; it was set into regular figure-of-eight flutes, and provided a frame for faces, both male and female. Great variety was apparent in masculine leg-wear. Old-fashioned, padded trunk-hose were often given differently patterned, tight extension pieces (**canions**) to cover the hiatus between their lower edge and the tops of the stockings.

'**Venetians**' provided an alternative. These were true
breeches; pear shaped and falling to just below the
knee. At the same time German versions of the upper-
stocks had ever more voluminous linings pulled
through their '**panes**'. German women wore more
moderate farthingales than those now seen at the
Spanish and English courts; and covered the bodice
by flared, hip-length jackets with short puffed sleeves.
Italian dress, more moderate still, kept closer to a
natural form. Although there women's hips were
padded, stiff frames were seldom used. All over
Europe the most costly textiles were closely patterned
by regular arrangements of tiny **cuts** made by special
chisels.

Mannerism (1580–1600)

The cone- and bell-shaped farthingales had been a Spanish innovation in the 1460s which spread all over fashionable Europe in the 1550s when so many areas were subject to the Spanish crown. The farthingale employed in France by the 1580s gave a rather different effect. This was an oval frame, extending only from the waist to hip level where it reached its maximum dimension – the skirt dropping straight from its edge to the floor in the manner of a cloth spread over a table. The immensely long, sharply pointed bodice pushed the frame down at the front, tilting it up at the back. The width across the hip was balanced by huge sleeves, also supported by whalebone or **bombast**, and by the ruff – opened in front to stand like a fan about the shoulders.

Mannerism (1580–1600)

The male doublet at this time developed a drooping protuberance over the stomach, known as a **peascod-belly**. It was worn with every kind of leg-covering, including some hybrid forms combining Venetian breeches with vestigial padded trunk-hose. The parts of the suit continued to be united at the waist (invisibly) by points, as they had been for two centuries. On most occasions men wore a circular cape or cloak, sometimes having a collar and revers, sometimes equipped with dummy sleeves, proclaiming its ancestry in the flared houppelande or gown of earlier days. Hanging sleeves appeared on women's gowns and men's **jerkins** – an over-garment almost indistinguishable from the doublet, and worn throughout the century.

Mannerism (1570–1600)

It was during the later years of the 16th century that, at last, a much closer approximation to currently fashionable dress began to be worn outside the immediate ranks of the nobility and gentry. Although very simple cut and a moderate adaptation of the square shapes and the horizontal emphasis of fifty years earlier survived among the poorer peasants and labourers, yet, even in the country (in England, in particular, where already the strict demarcation between classes could be more easily crossed than elsewhere), prosperous yeomen and small farmers followed the smarter, more slender lines and paid greater attention to distinctive details very soon after these had appeared at court.

Breeches, although less full and less padded, were

recognizable kin to the definitive styles in town. Skirts, though not held into broad-based cones by hoops, were given some resemblance to the latest modish forms by better cutting, or the addition of petticoats and hip-pads. Farmers' wives, up for a day to sell produce, met the women from the families of citizens, merchants and retailers on a new level of visual equality. More men and women encircled their necks with carefully set ruffs – smaller but no less neat than those surrounding the faces of the highest aristocrats. But concessions to utility were naturally made, in loose, easily slipped-on jerkins and protective aprons, while the low necks of tightly laced bodices in the new style were modestly covered by starched and folded kerchiefs or filled by finely gathered shifts.

Mannerism (1600–1620)

Through the first twenty years of the 17th century adjustments to small details of dress gradually changed appearances radically. The hard, smooth lines, the strange contradictions and exaggerations, the sharp angularities of Mannerist expression were, little by little, softened and made less extreme. The wadded peascod-belly of the doublet disappeared. A decrease in over-all padding, and a shorter waist, less tightly constricted, restored a more natural proportion to the male torso. And although trunk-hose and pear-shaped breeches continued together in the fashionable wardrobe, the appearance of both was more yielding. The stuffing was left out and only a thick blanket-like interlining gave pliable fullness to the deep pleats.

Mannerism (1600–1620)

In every detail roundness was more and more notable – in the wider dressing of women's hair; in the deep oval cut of their *décolletage*; in the general replacement of sharp-edged farthingale frames by the gentler rotundity of a thick **'bum-roll'** (a circular pad very like a motor-tyre tied around the hips); and in the huge shoe 'roses' of stiffened, spangled lace which decorated the instep fastening-straps of the newly fashionable high-heeled shoes. Appearing first as low, solid, wedge-shaped elevators in the 1590s, heels often added approximately 2in. (5cm) to the height of men and women by 1610 – for as yet the shoes worn by both sexes were identical. Full scarf-like garters, tied below the male knee, added a flamboyant touch to stockings lavishly decorated with embroidered 'clocks'.

Baroque (1620–1640)

By 1625 the accumulation of small detailed changes had produced a visual style quite contrary to that of Mannerism. The waistline of the doublet was now very short; its old decorative border of overlapping tabs increased in size and depth becoming an essential skirt or basque. Soft, unpadded breeches fell to just below the knee, where frequently they met the wide bucket-tops of riding-boots. Now worn even by non-equestrian fashionables at all times, these were pushed down, wrinkling about the lower leg, and allowing the extravagant trimming of **boot-hose** to spill out. Collars left unstarched and unsupported spread over shoulders, and longer locks of hair hung down to curl elaborately over the heavy borders of linen-lace. Cloaks, no longer worn symmetrically, were slung

diagonally around the body, or might be 'allowed a covering for one elbow'.[1] Small, high-crowned hats had been replaced by lower crowns and broad brims loaded with sweeping plumes. Similar changes had been made to women's dress. Shorter waists; less padding; wide fan-shaped collars allowed to spread horizontally, or droop down around the shoulders; unpadded, but softly ballooning sleeves often (like those of men) left open on the inner seam to show the underwear or a fine lining; and the skirts of gowns tucked up to give a casual effect. All these touches had transformed Mannerism in dress into the expression called Baroque – just as in the other arts robustness and bravura replaced artificiality and strangeness.

From James Shirley's play *The Lady of Pleasure* (1635). 81

Baroque (1620–1640)

Coinciding with a new sensuality in all the arts, Baroque dress employed sumptuous textiles in ways which displayed their natural heaviness and draping qualities to best advantage. Thick satins – their surfaces often decorated by tiny cuts alternating with **spangles** – combined with gleaming velvets or the matt softness of fine, closely textured woollens. Such woven textiles harmonized with the natural smoothness of buff or glossed leather, much used for jerkins, jackets and cassocks as well as for boots. High waistlines, adopted by both sexes, allowed full play to the swinging movement given by deep pleating in skirt or breeches. Bold, easy gestures gathered up or slung massed drapery to catch the light in rippling folds. The lavish use of richly dimensional laces and a profusion of ribbons and

feathers added further animation to the moving figure.

The full majesty of early Baroque expression in painting and architecture had emanated from Rome and there had been used by the Church in its efforts to recall people to Catholicism in a Counter Reformation. But the tendency to a warmer, more naturally emotional involvement in life and art was evident throughout a Europe reacting to the icy intellectualism of Mannerist detachment. During the 1630s dress at the French and English courts reached an apogee of elegance; while the prosperous bourgeois burghers of the newly created United Provinces of Holland were showing that middle-class patronage could compete with aristocratic splendour.

Baroque (1620–1650)

The years between 1620 and 1660 were filled with violence. Almost every European country was wracked by war or revolution, and military details in masculine dress naturally assumed considerable importance. Attempts to create a strong political structure to support the renewed vitality of the Catholic faith met fierce resistance from the partisans of recently established reformed religions. Church and states, united in the assertion of the Divine Right of kings, were challenged by the new self-confidence of the middle classes, backed by an equally strict religious conviction in favour of the liberty of individuals. The last remnants of medieval tradition were everywhere faced by the advance guard of modernism in many different guises. In dress the *forms* of fashion

were more rapidly assimilated by a larger proportion of the population than ever before, but it was thrift as much as any dominating puritanism which dictated simplification in detail outside the courts. Lace, braid and ribbons were more sparingly used, but except among the most rigorously fanatical of the small minority groups there was as much colour to be seen as in the smartest circles. Crimson, scarlet and orange-tawny as well as the accents of gold trimming were as evident among the blacks, greys and browns of the upholders of England's Commonwealth as they were among the merchants and citizens of the Protestant Netherlands. Even among the majority the last long-surviving Gothic garments were soon to disappear, and the clothes of the poorest labourers to be constructed on newer lines.

Baroque (1650–1660)

Holland was the first of the communities to recover from the miserable afflictions disturbing the rest of Europe until the 1660s. Between 1650 and 1660 the small republic became a centre of the arts and sciences. Its mainly urban population of merchants and bankers exploited the vast profits of foreign trade – particularly those of the East India Company – to set standards for domestic luxury, comfort and cleanliness not surpassed elsewhere for centuries. For a short period now the dress of men and women everywhere seemed to pursue slightly contrary tendencies. While that of men acquired a final caricatured over-all volume and fluidity, that of women moved steadily towards a renewed rigidity and formalism.

Baroque (1650–1660)

The sole surviving garment from the Gothic world – the male doublet – was, by 1660, reduced to the most abbreviated of jackets, not even reaching to the waist, and frequently having only elbow-length sleeves. Beneath it the fullest shirt bloused luxuriously about the torso and arms. Breeches, made as wide, straight tubes during the 1650s, became at the end of that decade an immensely full-pleated but divided skirt (**petticoat-breeches**), elaborately decorated by hundreds of yards of looped ribbon. From below the breeches there emerged either the full borders of under-drawers, the full tops of over-stockings turned down above garters tied below the knee, or separate valances called **canons**, falling to the calf.

Baroque (1650–1670)

Cloaks – a very necessary adjunct to the tiny doublet – began generally to be worn symmetrically again across both shoulders, or were replaced by very loose knee-length riding **cassocks**. The mania for exuberant volume affected the hair as well as the dress. After 1660 huge **periwigs** (available since the 16th century, but until now worn only by the ultra-fashionable) soon became daily wear, supplying the luxuriant curls in which Nature is often deficient. During the 1640s the bodice of a woman's dress had gradually acquired the quality of a corset. Lengthened again to a deep point on the abdomen, it was shaped to force the breasts upwards towards the throat and had frequently up to ninety strips of whalebone stitched into its lining, in addition to a long horn or wood

busk at the front to keep it completely rigid.
The short sleeves, set in below the curve of the
shoulder, made raising the arms difficult. The full,
frilled sleeve of the shift showed at the elbow, and a
deep lace-edged collar often fell from the straight,
wide *décolletage* to the base of the breast-bone. Separate
skirts, made from straight breadths of fabric, were
closely cartridge-pleated at the waist; and bodice and
skirt (as well as the petticoat beneath) were laid out
with formal bands and borders of braid, galloon or
wide metallic lace. Hair, fastened into a knot on the
crown, was dressed wide in front (sometimes over
wires) to fall in corkscrew ringlets to the shoulder,
each side of a central parting. Muffs, masks and hoods
were worn out of doors.

Baroque (1670s)

In 1661 Louis XIV assumed full powers as the principal absolute monarch in Europe. His ministers, building on the firm basis laid earlier by the statesmanship of Cardinals Richelieu and Mazarin, assured a new economic ascendancy for the French which, together with the powerful personality of the king, helped to establish his court as the ultimate arbiter in matters of art, elegance and 'high' fashion. Formality rapidly affected masculine dress. By the 1670s the riding cassock, smartened into a coat, was cut close and slim, to extinguish the Baroque exuberance of the breeches, now gathered into the knee, and their volume already much reduced. Low-placed pockets in the coat emphasized length, and only vents at sides and back eased its narrow cut for riding.

Baroque (1670s)

The abbreviated doublet was in general replaced by a **vest** – cut exactly like the coat and worn beneath it. Although wide-fringed and embroidered **baldricks**, shoulder-knots of ribbon, fringed, gauntletted gloves and ever more luxuriant wigs continued Baroque display, a generally neater, more disciplined air reflected the precise ceremonial of court etiquette. The female silhouette, retaining its rigid boned body, also grew slimmer, but at last a move was made to relieve women's dress from masculine domination. While the whalebone body and formal court dress continued to be constructed by a male tailor, a new kind of outer robe – the *manteau* or **mantua** – began to be made by women. Rapidly adopted by all classes, it laid the foundation for the later total division of fashion for the sexes.

Baroque (1675–1680)

The dress of the middle classes (although now so much more closely related to current high fashion) very naturally tended towards a conservative moderation, and to feature more obviously utilitarian details. The slightly older-fashioned boned bodice would have its *décolletage* covered by a short, lace-trimmed shoulder-cape (worn by the fashionable only during the toilet); the skirt of a best dress would be turned up in front, its hem pinned to the waist so that, if soiled, the marks would be concealed inside when the skirt was unpinned for the reception of visitors. But individual personality could always make its effect in the dashing angle of a hat, the swagger of an open coat or, conversely, in more formal care and grooming.

Baroque (1675–1680)

In fashionable society the mantua – at first a full-length informal boudoir gown, loosely pleated about the shoulders – was soon smartened for public appearances by catching the fullness close to the body in neat vertical pleats, fitting it over the underlying corset. The pleats, released from stitching below the waist, allowed ease in the trained skirt which, being open in front, was usually looped back with brooches or ribbon-knots to display the decorated petticoat. The bodice of the mantua, fastened in front by a number of ribbons tied in bows, later formalized as the **échelle**. Heads were covered by ribbon-trimmed caps with a deep frill of lace framing the face, the whole surmounted by a short veil falling on to the shoulders.

Baroque (1650–1680)

The dress of servants, city workers and farm labourers was at a still further remove from high fashion than was that of the more prosperous merchants, traders and professional people, but not in essential principles. Fashionable style filtered down to lower levels. Broad-brimmed hats, the turning-up and pinning-back of skirts, the shape of a sleeve or cuff, a smartly cut shoe, cast off by a noble lady and given to a maid; such items helped to link the classes. Though some details from an earlier age, like shoulder-wings at the sleeve head, or the wide turned-down 'band' or collar, continued as part of home-made or village-produced garments, city dwellers would be more likely to appear in clothes more recently fashionable.

Garments that were threadbare, patched or grubby might be second, third or sixth hand, but would have started from smarter circles, gradually descending the social scale as they lost their modishness. In any group specific contributions from the 'people' would be evident: straw sun-hats, loose smocks, rough wooden shoes, neat honeycomb stitching holding the fullness of an apron. Particular tools of a trade or craft – a shepherd's crook, a pitch-fork, a whetstone, a woman's distaff and spindle – would sometimes be carried or attached to a girdle. Individual street-vendors of every sort carried goods in a basket on the arm, or in a tray balanced on a pad on the head.

Baroque (1680–1715)

Modes emanating from the court of France in the 1690s set standards for the fashionable throughout Europe. Their architectural effect reflected the sumptuous splendour and ceremonial grandeur of Versailles. Trailing mantuas, their skirts opulently heaped behind on to **culs de Paris**, exposed rich petticoats thickly encrusted with gold braid, lace, embroidery, re-embroidered brocade, itself trimmed yet again with deep bullion fringes, cords and tassels. Aprons of lace or silk, ruched, beribboned, tasselled and fringed, were worn mainly for decorative effect. The head was ornamented by the '**fontange**' or '**commode**' – a lace cap with long lappets, its front border wired to stand as a high, pleated tower leaning well forward, and backed by loops of stiffened ribbon.

Baroque (1680–1715)

The coat of the masculine suit, still tightly waisted, now had widely spreading, stiffened skirts, enormous turned-back cuffs, and low-set pockets – deeply flapped, if horizontal, or multi-buttoned, if vertical. All buttonholes, pocket flaps, cuffs and front borders were formally outlined by regular patterns of braid or galloon. The vest, generally of gold or multi-coloured silk brocade, had sleeves, tight to the wrist, or with deep cuffs turning out over those of the coat. Wigs, ever more voluminous, rose in curled peaks on each side of a centre parting and fell in elaborate ringlets on breast and back. Hats, cocked into a triangle, were feather fringed; **patches** became general. Huge muffs were carried, and overcoats called **Brandenburgs** added extra warmth in winter.

Baroque (1680–1715)

As men's dress now settled into a new uniform appearance of coat, vest, knee-breeches and stockings, in place of doublet, hose, jerkin and cloak, so women's clothes settled into the regular arrangement of a mantua, its skirt opened in front and pinned behind, showing the petticoat beneath. Always with elbow-length sleeves, the bodice of the mantua appeared in two distinctive forms. The earlier – usual between 1675 and 1685 – had a *décolletage* open in a wide, shallow V to the middle of the breast-bone, from which point it closed to the waist by lacing or ribbon ties. The other – becoming generally fashionable after 1690 – was open to the waist in a deep, narrow V, exposing a **stomacher** (a triangular, embroidered panel) pinned

on to the front of the corset which would otherwise be visible. Both types of bodice-opening were bordered by a narrow turn-back revers called **robings.** Petticoats – floor-length, fashionably – were instep, ankle-length or even shorter among busy working women, just as the skirts of a workman's coat might reach only to mid-thigh instead of to the modish length, just below the knee. An informal cap with a fur-covered turned-up brim, cut into a V in front, worn only indoors by smart men, appeared in public among less dress-conscious males. The caps of ordinary women, though rising moderately in front, did not compete with the towering fantasy of the fashionable fontange. Children continued to be dressed as tiny adults.

99

Rococo (1720–1730)

From the beginning of the 18th century there was evidence of changing attitudes to art, life and manners, seen first most effectively in France. Bored by stately formality, grand solemnity and the rigorously prescribed routine of Versailles' etiquette, even Louis XIV in his declining years favoured a more delicate style of interior design, using soft colours and lighter filigreed carving. After the old king's death in 1715, the court moved thankfully back to the small Parisian hôtels and apartments around the palace of the regent, the pleasure-loving Duc d'Orléans. A new leisurely informality, a domesticated relaxation of behaviour was reflected in all the arts, and particularly in the luxuries of life, including furnishings and dress. Until 1715 the relaxation was gradual, but before 1720

the new style, now called 'Rococo', was clearly forming. In reaction to the old order, boudoir dress was
now worn in public. The pleats and gathers on
shoulders and back of the mantua were left to hang
loose, and this robe, now given such names as **sack**,
sacque, **robe volante**, **contouche**, etc, spread over
the still corsetted torso without defining it, to balloon
about the swaying bell of a hooped petticoat. Modest
in size when newly reintroduced about 1710, the hoops
increased enormously during the 1720s. Lustrous
satins or crisp rustling taffetas, in delicate opalescent
colours, were left almost undecorated. In contrast to
the stiff fontange, a tiny frilled lace cap, its lappets
pinned up, was worn above shorter hair dressed in
bubbling curls.

Rococo (1725–1730)

Although in England the hooped petticoat tended to be more angular in its outline, and bodices to be much more clearly defined than in France, sack-backs to mantuas were fashionable, and all the smaller details of French dress were instantly emulated. Similar modifications were made to masculine clothing. The elaborate, braided garnish was gradually discarded to leave only a narrow border of lace, laid on at the front edges of the coat and around cuffs and pocket-holes – though even this might not be used. Seemingly complementary to the spreading skirts of female gowns, the skirts of male coats gradually acquired more and more fabric on each hip, its fullness held by a button.

Rococo (1725–1730)

Before the 1720s were over, as much as a complete semi-circle of cloth was set into fan-pleats on each side of the male coat and, in addition, the skirts were interfaced with linen and horsehair, or even wired to produce the admired balletic flair. Pocket flaps and cuffs continued deep and bold, though wigs were much reduced in volume. Their variety was manifold, but the general tendency was towards shortish front and sides arranged in horizontal rolls, the long back hair plaited, or in ringlets tied back by ribbon. Three-cornered hats were the rule, also gradually moderating in size. The shoes of men and women were now markedly differentiated – women's high-heeled and pointed-toed, men's low-heeled and round-toed, both buckled on the instep.

Rococo (1740–1760)

The brilliant character of French society, centred on court and town, was formed in the *salon*, dominated by intelligent women. The more sober English society, based in many magnificent new country houses, was focused, when in town, around the exclusively masculine clubs. These differences of interest and temperament were evident in the dress of the two nations, and began to mark a divergence between the main centres of fashion, those for women being inspired primarily by French dressmaking, those for men increasingly set in London, but having strongly rural overtones. Even by the 1740s cloth was more in evidence than silk for masculine wear, although the waistcoat, delicately embroidered, frequently continued to provide a reminder of former satin splendours. The **frock**, an informal shooting-coat with

narrower skirts and a turned-down collar, grew in favour for **undress** wear. At the same time the fronts of the coat began to be curved away to display the shortening waistcoat and tightening breeches. Most men continued an earlier fashion for dressing the wig's long back hair in a black silk bag, but some younger men had grown their own hair again, more naturally arranged. Country hats with low crowns and wide brims began to appear in town. English women generally preferred the close-backed mantua, its body laced over a stomacher, its skirt open to show a petticoat. This 'suit' might be embroidered in a variation on the traditional flowering 'Indian tree' design, worked in bright, fresh colours on a neutral ground; or a simple, quilted petticoat gave a rustic touch.

Rococo (1760–1770)

Despite many extraordinary and outrageous fashions, 18th century dress in fact offers much evidence to justify the claim that this was the 'Age of Reason' and of 'Enlightenment'. During the late 1750s attempts were being made to come to terms with the natural mental development of growing children. In 1762 J. J. Rousseau's treatise on education – thinly disguised as a novel, *Emile* – brought into wide popular notice ideas already advocated in the 17th century by the English philosophical reformers Sir Francis Bacon and John Locke. The time at last seemed ripe to allow even some possibility of a more natural *physical* development too, and advanced mothers, under Rousseau's guidance, abandoned the swaddling of babies and began to moderate the rigidity of clothing for older children.

Simpler frocks and shorter hair began the cautious movement towards a liberation of the body, soon to be accelerated by a desire for Liberty as a general principle. Meanwhile, during the second half of the 18th century, several important developments marked the beginnings of an evolution of the old *craft* of adult dress into the modern *art* of *haute-couture*. Firstly it was in the 1760s and '70s that the work of *modiste* (*see* Glossary) and *milliner* began to assume prominence. Although the tailor continued to make the corset and the whalebone body of a court dress, and the mantua-maker to construct the robe and petticoat, while the seamstress produced lingerie, each according to traditional methods, the modiste and milliner – unhampered by Guild regulations (*see* Glossary) or craft

Rococo (1760–1770)

conservatism – could be imaginatively inventive in devising trimmings for female dress, and innovating new accessories. From this time increasingly it was *mouvementé* decoration applied to the surface of dress which caught the eye and gave it a *cachet*. Woven patterns and embroidery declined in favour. Dimensional ornament frequently composed from several different materials was preferred. This was at first confined to a mixture of ribbon loops and bows, and pinked and scalloped furbelows or flounces of self-fabric which was also used for narrow bands of **ruching**. But it was not long before box-pleated 'butterfly' ribbons, gathered lace, fringes, strings of beads, artificial flowers, cords and tassels, bands of fur, puffs of gauze and padded **plastic ornaments** were

used, frequently together, in a frivolous *mélange*, to give a new, exaggerated femininity. Lace ruffles at the elbow increased in lightness, depth and number. These **engagéantes**, originally attached to the shift, were now sold as separate items by the modiste and tacked into the dress. Millinery – based at first on utilitarian country straw hats with wide, round brims – soon began to assume a totally decorative and often fantastic effect, loaded with assorted trimming, and placed on top of a **mob-cap** equally fantastic and elaborate. The art of the hairdresser too rose – literally – to a peak of extravagance unknown before, as hair was piled ever higher over pads and caked with pomatum and powdered. But as women increased the complexity of their dresses men began to simplify their garments.

Rococo (1750–1780)

While the aristocratic and the wealthy were 'inventing' childhood and transforming fashionable dress from a craft devoted to public display of social distinction into an art of frivolous competitive private luxury for individuals, England was the scene of social changes eventually to have far-reaching effects throughout Europe. Due to the rapid acceleration after 1760 of an old system of enclosing common-land to form private estates, small holders and yeomen almost disappeared – demoted either to farm labourers or migrating to become city workers. Unparalleled agricultural improvements on the vast estates had a counterpart in mechanical inventiveness in industrial method, and a sudden increase in population provided the newly forming factory system with innumerable

'hands'. The interdependence of coal-mine, steel-yard and textile-mill was established, and growing cities and 'landscaped' estates were changing the face of the country. Ironically the 'Age of Enlightenment' was also the period in which the great division between Capital and Labour was made, and a chasm opened up between the two ends of the social scale. And yet equally ironically it was a time in which the farmer's smock-frock and his wife's sun-bonnet provided the nearest approach to a folk-costume ever seen in England. While, in other respects, those outside high society or ambitious middle class considerably adapted fashionable forms in dress to their particular requirements, fashionable *details*, only slightly out of date, continued to spice the most modest turn-out.

Rococo (1770–1780)

But a little consideration of the dress of even the highest society will show that by the 1770s a new 'levelling' spirit was having its effect. While formal court dress continued on the established lines of whalebone body and an oval hooped skirt – which could measure as much as 5ft (1.5m) from side to side, and only 18in. (46cm) from front to back – new forms of daily dress were making inroads into the old hieratic tradition. Fashionably, the short-skirted petticoat of the working woman was adopted for informal occasions, while long robes tucked up *à la polonaise* or *circassienne* imitated the way in which a serving girl had for thirty years trussed up the skirts of her mantua into the **pocket-holes**.

Rococo (1770–1780)

Alternatively, the robe was dispensed with altogether to be replaced by a **caraco jacket** or **pet en l'air**, with fitted bodice and short pleated basque – the descendant of the linen domestic bodice peasant women had worn since the 16th century. These dresses were often made in painted calico instead of brocaded silk, increasing their domestic air while suggesting a fanciful rusticity. Men's clothes grew simpler still. Complete suits in a self-coloured broad cloth were not unusual and, to the sleek lines of closer moderate cut, many sporting touches, like riding-boots or leather breeches worn in town, began to justify the complaints of the elderly that younger men dressed like grooms or coachmen. The heads of both sexes provided a final, defiant flourish of rococo fantasy.

Neo-classicism (1780–1795)

The frivolous spirit of the rococo in the decorative arts was gradually modified from the 1770s onwards by a return to a more severe Neo-classicism, and this classical spirit began to affect dress too by the 1780s – though frivolity was by no means entirely past, and feminine headgear grew **more expansive** and magnificently beplumed. But the close-backed English robe became the height of Parisian fashion and trimming was reduced to the minimum. The generation first put into children's frocks in the 1760s were adults by the '80s, and many grown women took to simple one-piece muslin morning gowns *à la mode anglaise* or *à la mode créole* with draw-strings at neck and waist, worn with a wide silk sash.

Neo-classicism (1780–1795)

Hip-padding was much reduced, waists were raised, and full neckerchiefs, crossed at the bust and tied behind, added to the childlike air. All this change was the outward sign of the thinking which was to erupt in the French Revolution with the storming of the Bastille in 1789, but it was evident long before, even among the highest aristocracy. Marie Antoinette dressed *à la mode créole* at Trianon before 1783 and ordered many new dresses in the simpler styles for the flight to Varennes in 1791. Yet gay society continued to promenade extravagantly dressed through the arcades of the Palais Royal until the execution of Louis XVI in 1792. Smart Frenchmen wore fancifully caricatured versions of English riding dress cut very tight.

Neo-classicism (1795–1800)

During the period of the Terror in France, between October 1793 and the establishment of the Directory in August 1795, only the simplest dress was safe. But, by then, extremely simple dress was general in Europe. The Neo-classical spirit of liberty and equality had been everywhere effective. Once the worst excesses of the Revolution were passed, however, relief found its expression in an outbreak of fantasy and extravagance. The raffish group of opportunists, always the obvious survivors in times of crisis, indulged in extremes: short **frock-coats** with vast lapels, several waistcoats, deep **cravats**, like neck-bandages rising above the chin, unkempt hair and thin, pointed pumps for men, whose clothes seemed at once too small and yet too big.

Neo-classicism (1795–1800)

The width, which had characterized women's dress from 1720–1785, was now replaced by length. Waists rose almost to the armpit, and trains were often so long that they could be draped over the arm without exposing more than the ankle. Until 1800 several petticoats and a pad continued to be worn by the majority, only the really extreme minority appearing in a single muslin shift worn over a garment of skin-tight, flesh-pink knitted silk, simulating nakedness. Long scarves and shawls added a classical touch to dresses occasionally imitative of antique modes, but these appeared incongruously with enormous muffs and wildly beribboned bonnets – though 'heads' were growing smaller.

Neo-classicism (1795–1805)

Neo-classicism was one aspect of the romantic mood gaining in strength during the closing years of the 18th century. The idea that total liberty and equality could be achieved was itself a romantic ideal. The close imitation of ancient architecture, furnishing and dress was equally romantic. While a few women carried such imitation to a logical conclusion, wearing sandals and Greek or Roman hair-styles, already by 1804, when Napoleon proclaimed himself Emperor of France, historical details from other ages began to soften a short-lived severity. Frills, ruffles, bows, puffed sleeves and Turkish turbans were mixed with Grecian **peplums**, Roman borders and tiaras and feathered, helmet-like bonnets. The popularity of sheer delicate muslins made pockets impractical and large **reticules**

became a necessity. Parasols and York-tan gloves detracted too from a pedantic revivalism by their novel modernity. Men never forsook the present for a fanciful past, although very short waistcoats demanded that pantaloons be cut very high in the rise and this, together with their usual pale colour, displayed the lower limbs in an almost deceptively antique manner. Coats were cut back in front well above the waist leaving long tails behind. More advanced were 'frocks' – double-breasted and closed evenly all round. Both varieties of coat had aggressive lapels and very high, padded collars. Younger men *did* sport hair-cuts *à la Brutus*, and narrow-brimmed, high-crowned top-hats began to replace all forms of tricorn or cocked hats.

Romantic 1800–1815

The combination of light-weight, often transparent textiles with increasingly pretty but fussy detail had gradually been helping to create a new conception of Woman as a fragile ethereal being, in keeping with the angelic spirituality and inaccessibility emphasized by the young generation of poets and novelists. Women's dress was now made entirely by female dressmakers, and it had begun to be thought improper for men to be aware of the more intimate garments in the female wardrobe. High waists and a slim silhouette continued until 1815 or so, but satins and velvets returned to fashion after 1804, at least for outer garments such as the **pelisse** and for evening dresses, while the assortment of exotic and multi-historical details became increasingly fanciful and flamboyant. As women took on an ever more exaggerated effect

of helpless 'femininity' so men grew more complementary in their stronger 'masculinity'. Racy clothes
reflected racy manners and the years of the Napoleonic
wars introduced a certain military swagger even to
civilian dress. **Hessian boots, pantaloons** decorated
with scrolled Hungarian braiding, and multi-buttoned
or 'frogged' coats, all combined with dark or strongly
coloured cloth, and pale buckskin or **nankeen**, to
differentiate men very markedly from their women-
folk, as did shorter hair, side-whiskers, top-hats and an
increasing vogue for trousers (in a variety of shapes)
on informal occasions. Coats, however, *were* still cut
very close, with narrow sloping shoulders and a little
fullness gathered at the sleeve-head; frilled shirts and
embroidered silk waistcoats *still* appeared.

Romantic 1800–1815

Inevitably at a time when high fashion had scaled down its effects and was concentrating upon simplicity of line and textiles, the clothing worn by working people fitted more closely to the current ideal than was possible when sumptuous fabric and exaggerated form had been the minority mode. Yet even so, dress on the farm, in the factory, or seen upon the street-traders of the increasingly large and increasingly dirty cities had a character of its own. Coarse calico and drill was used instead of fine muslin or lawn. Rough tweed or hop-sack appeared instead of broadcloth or smooth melton. 'Shoddy', the name given to a cheap cloth made by reweaving the wool of old garments, and 'sleasey' (a flimsy lawn) have become synonymous with poor quality.

The trade in second-hand garments developed to the proportion of an industry and the poorer folk were recognizable, as in any age, by their assemblage of chance finds in haphazard combinations; by repairs and patches; and whether clean or dirty, by threadbare areas at all natural points of stress – elbows, knees and buttocks. The **spencer**, a short, bob-tailed coat worn after 1790 in smart circles for extra warmth, was, because of its economy of cloth, a gift for the impoverished. Both male and female versions united the fashionable and the unfashionable. The proletariat had also set *one* fashion – trousers – gradually making its way *up* instead of down the social scale.

Romantic 1815–1820

After the final collapse of the First Empire in 1815 Europe was left without any single focus for especial display. Real power was now concentrated in the hands of a new polygenous group – the bourgeoisie. Under this heading were concentrated not only the traditional middle class of merchants, bankers, and professional people, but a wide spectrum of society, from the most magnificent industrial magnates or army contractors to people whose speculative investments during the crisis years had given them a few hundred pounds and a minimum of education, raising them above the 'workers' upon whom they could look down. This now vast middle class was itself dividing into upper, middle and lower sections.

The years from 1815 to 1852, with their 'gentility' – although in general tone Romantic – may best be classified as *Biedermeier*. This satirical title, derived from the German words *bieder* (upright, honest) and *meier* (a steward or dairy farmer), has been accepted by scholars as epitomizing comfortable homely qualities together with a decorative style rich, massive and derivative, which provided the ideal for the ubiquitously influential middle classes, the latest arbiters of elegance during this period. 'Neo-classical' in general inspiration, 'Empire' in sumptuosity, 'Romantic' in its references to any and every historical epoch, women's dress continued to accumulate fine but fussy dressmakers' details – men's to become increasingly 'respectable'.

Romantic 1820–1830

Voluminous, satin-lined, tassel-trimmed capes or many-caped greatcoats gave a highly romantic image to those men who covered sober velvet-collared coats and baggy trousers in their swinging folds. But this vogue owed as much to practicality as to Romanticism, since the full effect of 'macadamizing' main roads was adding impetus to the speed and frequency of coach travel. Before 1820 the waistline of women's dress was beginning to drop again, year by year, reaching its natural position at least by 1824. This development was accompanied by the return in full force of the corset. Unlike earlier whalebone bodies new **stays** were very curved, and constructed to control hips as well as waist and bust.

The silhouette now resembled an hour-glass instead

of an inverted cone. As pressure at the waist increased so (to give by optical illusion the appearance of an impossibly small measurement) fullness was added above and below between 1820 and 1829. From that date small down-filled pillows were required to inflate huge sleeves, and overlying **epaulettes**, **mancherons** and deep '**Berthas**' emphasized width across the shoulder. Balance was kept by widening the ever-shortening skirt – at first with gores, then by holding out the hemline with padded bands, cords or applied three-dimensional decoration. Petticoats multiplied and small **bustles** added further volume. Wide bonnets and hats decked with foaming plumes and fluttering ribbons completed the effect of a rather over-dressed doll.

Romantic 1830–1835

Through logical evolution the sleeves of women's dresses reached an illogical maximum by 1832. Set in below the curve of the shoulder, on to the upper-arm, they tended (together with extra shoulder capes) to exaggerate a steeply sloping line from the elaborate ruffled collar encircling the throat to the widest point across the figure, from elbow to elbow. Feet (markedly visible since hems were at instep or ankle level) were shod in the tiniest, narrowest, flexible heelless shoes or satin boots – the ancestor of the modern ballet-slipper. The ballerina – apparently weightless – began to dance 'on point' and the fashionable dress of the 1830s formalized into the classical costume for *La Sylphide*, a fitting symbol for the delicate airy sprite which was the poetic ideal at this peak of Romanticism.

Romantic 1830–1835

The equally romantic male – eternally dancing attendance on his coyly blushing, timid counterpart – presented a dashing figure. His frock-coat (thrown wide open with huge revers and an immensely deep, rolling, padded collar) was nipped smartly in at the waist and full in the skirt. His trousers (or 'unmentionables') were skin-tight about hips and thighs, flaring at the foot into a bell almost covering his lacquered boots to their square-tipped toes. Several flower-sprigged waistcoats and a frilled shirt decorated his broadly masculine chest. Curly hair, with luxuriant side whiskers, was crowned by a tall shiny hat. Though colours were generally darker there remained immense variety in *form* for men – particularly in outer wear.

Romantic 1835–1840

After 1836 huge ballooning sleeves collapsed – declining first into puffs, ruffs or ruches around the biceps. But the newer, tighter sleeve was still set in very low to keep the long sloping 'bottle-shouldered' line, so complementary to the extremely curvaceous bodice. Skirts, no longer gored but very closely cartridge-pleated at the waist, continued to increase in volume as interest was lost in sleeves. Bonnets were pulled in more closely to the chin and most of the fluttering detail and overloaded flouncing disappeared in favour of a neater, restrained line. Throughout the 1830s and '40s the vogue in textile design was for small sprigged patterns with a late 18th century flavour – and many original 18th century dresses were remade in the latest shapes.

For people with modest purses or no inherited brocades there were inexpensive cottons printed in minute floral or geometric designs. Pieces from these doll-sized patterns may still be identified among the hexagonal scraps in many patchwork quilts. It was not yet fashionable for men to wear matched coat, waistcoat and trousers so the 'assorted' look of the impecunious was no sure identification – only the fit and the condition of garments was a certain guide. Tophats (fashionably very varied in shape) were worn by all classes, but usually caps with puffy crowns and stiff shiny peaks were worn by small boys, students, sporting characters, and those without pretension to high fashion.

Romantic 1835–1850

Changes in feminine appearances which had begun in about 1836 evolved into the characteristic silhouette of the '40s – long and slender of body, full in the skirt, small and neat at the head. Bonnets reduced in size, their brims closed closely about the face in a deep inverted U during the '40s, widening into a more open circular shape by 1850. Skirts lengthened again to the floor. Padding, layers of petticoats (occasionally an 'Arctic' petticoat of quilted down) and stiffening with **crinoline** (a fabric woven from horse-hair and linen) produced the typically rounded bell-like line. Hair, brushed smoothly from a centre parting, fell in drooping ringlets. The very curved shoulder line and 'poking' carriage of the head helped to emphasize an

effect of dragging weight and a slightly invalidish air. The waistline of a man's coat was lengthened to give a more solid, heavy look to the torso, and faces became increasingly hirsute as the period progressed. Otherwise there was little notable change, except the continued progress towards darker uniformity. Although children's clothing had never returned to a pre-18th century rigidity, considerable similarity to adult dress was evident once more. Small boys wearing puffed-sleeved, belted tunics and wide white collars could easily be mistaken for girls, except for their short hair and pantaloons. Slightly older boys were dressed in 'skeleton suits', with tight short jackets and close-fitted trousers finishing above the ankle.

Romantic 1845–1855

The extreme difficulty of getting an outer-coat over the huge female sleeves of the 1830s and the voluminous skirts of the '40s meant that shawls were universal. Originally an expensive but somewhat inappropriate accessory in the 18th century when they had been imported from Kashmir, the classical mania of the early 19th century gave them greater meaning and popularity as added 'antique' drapery, and had led to their European imitation. From 1803 Norwich shawls were woven with Kashmir patterns, to be followed by those from Paisley after 1808. A prized possession throughout the first half of the century, these fringed rectangles, folded cornerwise, and wrapped around the body, 'covered all deficiencies' for those whose dresses were not quite in the latest mode.

Fashionably the shawl or a long scarf was draped just on the bend of the shoulder, and seemed to bind the arms to the body, adding one more touch to the admired appearance of helplessness. *Unfashionably* they turned the wearer into a shapeless bundle! A certain gaiety in striped, checked and tartan textiles became evident as the '40s merged into the '50s, enlivening men's trousers, and particularly children's dresses. These continued very bi-sexual for the younger age-group, the hat and hair frequently presenting the only distinction. And in the matter of broad-brimmed, low-crowned hats, little girls were again in advance of their still bonneted mama's by some few years.

Romantic 1850–1860

Hats *were* worn by grown women, but were considered rather 'fast' on married heads. The 1850s produced a far more flamboyant and mature-looking woman. The volume of the skirt was constantly increased by adding more and more petticoats – then by the optical illusion of layers of horizontal frills and trimming. After about 1856 even bigger and better skirts became possible with the introduction of the 'cage' or 'artificial crinoline'. This mass of flexible watch-spring steel hoops suspended on tapes allowed a huge circumference but lessened weight. Wider skirts required higher waists, and bodice trimming tended to sweep across broader bosoms. Sleeves widened to the wrist, echoing the line of the skirt, and colours grew even more strident.

Romantic 1850–1860

The Great Exhibition in London in 1851 and the establishment of a Second Empire in France in 1852 marked a change of mood in the century. Although still essentially romantic in its mania for the past and in its faith in progress towards a glorious future, a new, rather vulgar materialism was abroad. The results of industrialization, world-wide commerce and conquest were making their mark in the quantity and variety of fabric used in fashionable female dress, and the complexity of its trimming. Women were walking advertisements for their husband's bank balance, but men seemed set towards utility and comfort. Frock-coats remained *de rigueur* for town, but 'lounging' jackets, easy in cut, with short skirts, and worn with low-crowned 'wide-awake' hats, appeared on all off-duty moments.

Romantic 1860–1870

The **crinoline cage**, at first a symmetrical dome, was soon flattened in front to leave all fullness sweeping magnificently to sides and back. Overskirts, drawn up for convenience in outdoor exercises such as archery or croquet, and for wear on the beach, suggested a new possibility, and before the decade was over this romantic reminder of the 18th century polonaise had started another transformation. In 1858 Charles Frederick Worth, born in Lincolnshire, trained in London and employed in France, opened a 'dress-establishment' in Paris and *haute-couture* was born. Commissioned in 1860 to dress the Empress Eugénie, this artist now offered a completely designed ensemble which could be purchased like a picture or a vase. While feminine extravagance was becoming synony-

mous with 'fashion', men continued on a downward path to dullness. Heavy-looking torsos were supported on solid shapeless columns – trousers being cut wide and 'peg-topped', entirely disguising the shape of the leg. Sack-like **Tweedside** and other 'lounging' jackets became ever more usual, and occasionally a 'business suit' of 'dittos' (cut all from one cloth) made its appearance. Bowler-hats were introduced for undress wear and were sometimes seen in town. Faces became hairier than ever, a favourite growth being very long side whiskers known as **Dundrearies**. By 1867 women abandoned the bonnet in favour of piled-up hair-styles and forward-tilted hats, reminiscent, like their dresses, of the fashions of a hundred years earlier.

Romantic 1870–1880

Haute-couture did not die with the Second Empire in the Franco-Prussian War of 1870. Paris rapidly recovered from its siege, Worth flourished, and dress during the 'sensuous 'seventies' was even more dashingly, luxuriantly magnificent than ever before. The crinoline had given place to the **crinolette** (a kind of half crinoline) which developed into the **dress-improver** (a frame supporting only the back of the skirt). Still 18th century in *inspiration*, the expensive *toilette* was far more complex and elaborate than anything *that* century had ever conceived – and far more voluptuous. Dress – like the other arts – had been released from an ancient dependence on *élite* nobility. Its latest patrons were plutocrats rather than aristocrats.

Even the most important innovation in painting – Impressionism – was concerned in subject matter with the luxurious materialism of the modern world, not with an imagined romantic past. Art – including dress – was fast becoming an expression of individual personality rather than that of a small enclosed 'society', while the sewing-machine, paper patterns and 'fashion' magazines helped to open up the possibilities of sartorial competition to increasing numbers. By 1876 the dress-improver was already old-fashioned and skirts were 'tied back' – dragged tightly across the thighs and bundled up under the buttocks, though no less material and detail was used. But the incongruous introduction of 'tailor-made' jackets above elaborate 'dressmaker' drapery in skirts heralded further change.

Romantic 1880–1890

The pace of change in fashionable female dress reflected rapid readjustments in society. Women were working – as journalists, telegraph operators and teachers, and taking active part in sports. Dress divided against itself into the tailor-made and the essentially frivolous – either being worn by the same women on different occasions. The narrow dragged and draped effects of the late 1870s were short lived, and a **bustle** – as brisk, businesslike and waggling as its name suggests – jutted smartly out at a sharp angle from 'the lower back', achieving a maximum projection by 1885. Hats like inverted flower-pots were worn straight on top of closely frizzed hair. The whole appearance was hard and angular, in keeping with the emergence of a new conception of Woman – rival and competitor rather than complement and consolation.

Men – except the most dandified – were rapidly abandoning formality for the 'lounge-suit'. Cut narrower with tiny revers and worn closely buttoned, it appeared with a high, hard, 'stick-up' shirt collar and was worn with a bowler-hat or 'boater' even in the smartest places. But the subtle, inch by inch changes in the masculine wardrobe were discernible only to a practised eye, paling into insignificance before fast, all too obvious and total transformations affecting women, season by season, at almost every social level. The tables had been turned, and although masculine *couturiers* like Worth, Creed and Doucet continued to produce influential offerings, it was now women who chose between them, deciding their own appearance.

Romantic 1880–1890

Vast wealth for some – and some money for many – was of course dependent upon a great mass of impoverished and underprivileged labourers for whom 'fashion' meant little beyond what other people could enjoy. The working classes – still the majority – were probably farther removed from the fashionable ideal (now that that ideal had become so extravagantly dynamic) than at any earlier time. *Haute-couture*, fashionable for a few months, had nothing much to do with people who might still – and almost certainly did – wear the same clothes day and night for a quarter of a century. The most obviously useful items from the fashionable wardrobe *were* adapted: short 'lounge-jackets' for men, who never had time to lounge, wide trousers which made movement easier, and those

shawls for women, still 'covering all deficiencies' at a level where the deficiencies were so many and so plain – a function shared for children by the pinafore which gave some protection to hardly won garments all too easily spoiled in dirty tenements and factories. Smocks and aprons, those ancient symbols of servitude, were unchanging. But curiously the navvy in his moleskin waistcoat and corduroy trousers wore a smart high-crowned bowler while mending the road. And although crinolines or bustles seldom appeared in this work-a-day world, a coster woman prized her 'fashionable' hat with its feathers and velvet bows, looking down on a still poorer woman whose bonnet was well out of date.

L'Art Nouveau 1890–1900

During the closing decade of the 19th century the decorative arts (more importantly than the fine arts) were being reassessed as a result of the consciously moralistic and mystic overtones of the Aesthetic and Arts and Crafts movements (active since the 1870s and '80s) and a quite new interest in the need for rational yet pleasing industrial design. Dress, too, was affected by these modern concerns. Fashionable dress was now a highly remunerative industry and an extremely personal art. The *couturier* had begun to live up to his name and the *cutting* of a dress was fast becoming the highest point for admiration. Even the complexity of the '70s had been achieved from relatively simple pieces, their final effect dependent upon deft draping and expert trimming.

But the skirt of the 1890s, fitting smoothly about the hips and developing by 1898 into a subtly shaped, sinuously fluid, flaring bell, was composed from many imaginatively shaped sections. There was a brief revival of interest in sleeves between 1890 and 1895, but from that date on 'line' was all important. The dichotomy of a woman's life was very evident in the smartly cut 'tailor-made' for working days (based upon skirt, jacket and shirt blouse) and the incredible confection of *satin charmeuse*, chiffon and lace for a garden-party, a theatre or a ball. Frivolous flower-decked hats were apt to crown a quite rational outfit for golf, tennis or the latest craze – bicycling – giving a clear indication of the equivocal attitude to the old life and the new.

Epilogue

The new life was to conquer . . . Women had begun in the late 1870s that course towards utility first undertaken by men exactly a century earlier in the late 1770s. The development of European dress into world dress belongs to the 20th century, and its relationship to the ever increasing complexity of influences from art and society requires a book to itself. Some indication of how truly world-wide European dress has become, at last, in the 1970s, may be given by a brief consideration of a not unusual, not too expensive collection of clothes. Restored, after just over a century of eclipse, to his rightful place as a being to whom dress may be allowed a proper interest, a man may include in his wardrobe underwear from one of the vast British chain stores (known to all Europeans), such as Marks and Spencer or C & A; shirts from Belgium, Switzerland or Sweden; a suit from Finland, West Germany or Holland; shoes from Spain; knitwear from Italy and perhaps a tie or two marked with the name of some prestigious Parisian Fashion House, as Yves Saint-Laurent or Nina Ricci. To add exotic ethnic spice from outside Europe, it could also contain cow-boy boots and blue jeans from the U.S.A., a Mexican poncho, an Arabian kaftan, a Japanese kimono, a fur hat from Russia and an embroidered coat from Afghanistan. There could be beads and pendants from Africa, and bangles, scarves and sandals from India. Cutting across class distinction, week-end wear might include a fisherman's sweater from Arran, a French workman's blouse and a genuine boiler suit from some industrial supply company, as well as a combat suit and duffle coat from a Government Surplus Store. The respectable daily suit from

Burton's may hang next to a far more expensively understated gala outfit from Cerruti, or something with more flamboyance from Tommy Nutter or Mr Freedom. A safari jacket for summer may alternate with ski (or *après-ski*) clothes for winter. The modern European is sartorially a man of the world – just as men (and women) all over the world are sartorially mainly European. Miscegenation seems to be the order of the day as far as clothing is concerned, although the very latest fashions (1975) look back not only into the recent past, but apparently longingly too at a certain nationalism. Perhaps after so long we need to rediscover our tribal identities again?

Glossary and Explanatory Notes

Arming-doublet, *see* **Doublet**

Baldrick A shoulder-belt worn diagonally from right shoulder to left hip. It could be used as a sword carriage, but could also be purely ornamental. They were very fashionable in the late 14th–early 15th centuries (sometimes decorated with bells), and again *c.* 1628–1700 when they were often very broad and richly embroidered and fringed.

Band or **ruff** A collar of linen. Originally it was the narrow frill projecting above the needlework which held the fullness of the body of shirt or shift into the neck. It assumed importance *c.* 1540 when it was allowed to show above the collar of the doublet. From *c.* 1565–*c.* 1580 it gradually increased in depth from about 1–9in. (2–23cm) or more, and during this time began at some point to be made as a separate article, to be pinned to the narrow straight neck-band of shirt or shift. Stiffly starched and set into symmetrical figure-of-eight flutes, it was tied together at the front by 'band-strings' decorated with small finial tassels. The band could be very elaborately decorated with black-work (q.v.), cut-work, lace at the edge and trimmed with pearls. When not in wear it was kept in a circular flat box – a band-box. From the late 16th century an alternative to this ruffled band was a flat, wide, fan-shaped collar sometimes called a 'whisk', but generally it kept the name 'band'. Early in the 17th century both the ruffled and flat collars were worn unstarched and were then known as 'falling bands'. After the introduction of full-bottomed periwigs, *c.* 1660, the band was reduced at the sides to leave square tabs falling on to the chest in front, these being eventually tied together by a ribbon bow *c.* 1665, and gradually discarded in favour of a cravat. A very modified and simple descendant of the 17th century development is retained as 'Geneva-bands' by ministers of some reformed churches.

Bertha   A deep falling collar, usually of lace, en-circling the low *décolletage* of a woman's bodice.

Black-work and **white-work**   Embroidery stitched in only black thread on a white ground, or in only white thread on a white ground. Black-work and white-work were particularly popular during the period between *c.* 1525–*c.* 1625, while white-work had a considerable revival in the 18th century.

Bombast   Stuffing of flocks, wool, bran, and other materials, used during the 16th and early 17th centuries to pad out breeches, sleeves, 'bum-rolls', etc., to achieve the admired inflation – hence the term 'bombastic' (inflated with senseless, high-sounding words).

Boot-hose   Over-stockings of linen, worn with riding-boots from *c.* 1535–*c.* 1680. Originally intro-duced to protect the fine silk stockings from oil and grease used to keep the leather of the boots supple, they quickly became an extra field for display, their tops being decorated with lace or fringes to fall out over the wide tops of the boots. Particularly prominent *c.* 1620–*c.* 1660.

Braies   Linen under-drawers worn by men in the Middle Ages. A descendant of the trousers worn by Persians and Scythians as well as by some tribes of northern barbarians, they were an alternative to bracae (breeches) in late Roman times (1st–5th centuries). Like loose pyjama trousers they were ankle length until the mid-12th century, being generally held close to the lower leg by bandages or by hose drawn over them. After the mid-12th century they were shortened to the knee, and then gradually reduced in volume until, by the late 14th century, they were much the shape and size of modern briefs. They were supported on the hip-bones by a cord, channelled through the top, and knotted in front. Until the early 14th century the hose were usually held up by being tied to this cord, gaps being left in the channelling on each side of the front for this purpose.

Brandenburg   A large, loose outer coat worn by men from *c.* 1670–early 18th century. It was cut like an outsize version of the fashionable coat, having deep turned-back cuffs and its buttons and buttonholes often decorated by 'frogging' or braid. The name derives from the Prussian city, famous at that time for a high-quality woollen much used for this garment.

Breeches (*See also* **Braies**)   First *general* use in Europe in late Roman times (1st–5th centuries). Called 'bracae', they were adopted by the military when on duty in outlying parts of the empire, only gradually infiltrating into daily civilian wear. In origin a northern tribal garment for men, probably first made by stitching together the skins from the hind parts of animals to form a covering for the loins and upper leg to just below the knee. Later made from woven fabric, looking like close, short pyjama trousers. They were unusual as a Roman civilian garment, until barbarian influences became strong in the empire in the 4th and 5th centuries, and were then in competition with trousers.

The term 'breeches' was first used in Britain in the late 16th century. They were seamed inside and outside each leg (unlike hose which had only one centre-back seam) and closed in front by four to five buttons, without a fly covering. Like hose they were at first trussed to the doublet by points, then (after *c.* 1625–30) hooked to it. From the mid-1630s they were self-supporting, the waistband being made tight enough to prevent them slipping over the hip-bones. The term was first applied indiscriminately to both true breeches (*see* **Venetians**) and trunk-hose (*see* **Hose**), but after the final disappearance of trunk-hose (*c.* 1625) breeches were the principal male nether garment until the end of the 18th century. There were many shapes and varieties. From *c.* 1570–*c.* 1640 they were generally full or narrow variations on an inverted-pear shape, being (if full) pleated on to the waistband and tapered towards the knee. From 1640 they were cut looser around the thigh hanging as straight tubes to knee level. During the 1650s the fullness was gradually increased, to form **petticoat-breeches** (a divided skirt) from the late 1650s to mid-1670s. After the general introduction of the coat (*c.* 1662) they were first gathered at the knee, then gradually narrowed again by the 1680s. By the early 18th century they were fitted fairly closely. From 1730 onwards they were cut tighter and tighter, the front fastening from that time being generally covered by a square flap ('falls') held up by buttons to the waist. When made very close to the leg, a slit at each side to about 5 in. (13cm) above the knee was necessary – closed by buttons and a strap and buckle. Most breeches had pockets. The French term for breeches – *culotte* –

appeared in the late 16th century, so that the defiant, plebian, trouser-wearing revolutionaries of the 1790s were known as *Sans-culottes* (those who do not wear breeches). In Germany the term *Hose* or *Hosen* was retained for breeches after the division of the hose into upper- and nether-stocks in the 16th century – so that the short Bavarian leather breeches are still *lederhosen*.

Brocade A textile, generally of silk thread, into which patterns have been woven on the loom in a variety of colours different from the ground. This is achieved by allowing only small sections of the coloured thread to appear on the surface where it is appropriate to the design, and then to 'float' behind when not needed for the figuring. Patterns may be large or small according to fashion, and may also include threads of gold, silver or silver-gilt as well as colour. Oriental in origin, brocades from Persia or China were highly fashionable in Europe from late Roman times, and Eastern influences on the design of brocades woven in Europe are evident until the 17th century at least. Important centres for the weaving of brocades in Europe were in Sicily (9th–13th centuries), particularly at Palermo (12th century); Lucca (13th–14th centuries); and Florence, Genoa and Venice (15th–17th centuries). During the 17th and 18th centuries France usurped the Italian lead, and French immigrant workers built up the important London industry at Spitalfields during the early 18th century. Spain had also produced brocades from an early date and continued to rival both Italy and France into the 19th century. By that date brocades woven from cotton or mixed threads were being produced everywhere in imitation of the more expensive silks.

Bum-roll (*See also* **Farthingale**)   A thick padded roll resembling a motor-tyre, tied together by tapes at the front. It was worn in the late 16th, early 17th centuries as an alternative to the farthingale, distending the skirts to a wide circumference at hip level, from which point they fell straight to the floor. It was also worn by men under full breeches which did not contain their own bombast.

Busk   A long narrow piece of horn, bone, wood or metal frequently triangular in section, used to hold the front of a bodice rigid. Extending from about the middle of the breast-bone to the pit of the stomach, the busk was sometimes quite straight, sometimes slightly concave, according to fashion. It fitted into a long narrow pocket specially constructed down the inside front of either bodice or corset, and was held in place by a 'busk-point' – a lace, which passed through eyelet-holes in the bodice, the base of the busk and the bodice-lining, and was then tied in a bow. In the 19th century the word lost much of its original meaning when any of the strips of whalebone or metal used to control the shape might be referred to as a busk.

Bustle   A small posterior pad intended to set off a skirt with full back pleats or gathers to the best advantage. They have been employed at various periods, notably during the 1680s and '90s to add to the effect of the looped back skirt of the mantua. They were then called 'cul-de-Paris'. Again during the 1770s and '80s they became very prominent as 'false rumps'. During the 1820s and '30s they became 'bustles' and at that time consisted of a pad covered with closely gathered flounces of 'crinoline'. Their last important appearance was between *c.* 1880 and *c.* 1889 when they were of very varied design but generally consisted of a light, flexible steel frame, sometimes equipped with elastic springs allowing them to fold up when the wearer sat down.

Canions Worn by men *c.* 1570–*c.* 1615, they were extension pieces to cover the hiatus over the thigh when trunk-hose were made very short and stockings reached only just above the knee. Like a section of old-fashioned long-hose they had a single back seam, were cut very close to the leg, and were stitched into the breeches' mouth. They were lined, and generally of quite different fabric, colour and pattern from the rest of the suit. Usually the tops of the stockings were drawn up over their lower end, but sometimes they were worn outside the stockings, covering them to just below the knee.

Canons Worn by men late 1650s–*c.* 1670. Fully gathered flounces of linen, lawn, or silk, sometimes lace edged, from 5–8in. (13–20cm) deep, tied on to each leg below the knee. They might match stockings or suit, and can be confused either with the deep turn-over top of boot-hose which has been gartered below the knee, or with a flounce falling from loose breeches or under-drawers worn with petticoat-breeches, and also tied below the knee.

Caraco One of a number of short jacket styles for women fashionable from *c.* 1750, particularly popular *c.* 1775–*c.* 1790. Front fastening and with a flared or pleated basque falling to about mid-thigh or shorter, they were worn with a short petticoat as a form of 'undress' at a time when informality was the vogue.

Casings (for the hair) During the 12th century fashionable young women wore their hair parted in the centre and plaited on each side. The pendant plaits were then encased in long silk sheaths (*fouriau*) rather like umbrella covers. Any deficiency in length of hair could be made up in length of sheath – its end padded out to add conviction.

Cassock From *c.* 1530, any coat-shaped, loose, short, wide-sleeved, utilitarian outer garment might be termed 'cassock'. From *c.* 1620 it was applied to a riding garment, fitted at the shoulder and flaring towards the hem, which varied from hip to thigh length. Often made with a back vent. Sometimes made to button on each side from armpit to hem, so that, unfastened, it hung like a tabard. This form was equipped with cape-shaped sleeves, also buttoning the full length from shoulder to wrist. It was possible therefore to unbutton the sleeves and button them to the open sides of the body to form a full cloak.[1] During the late 1640s it became usual to wear a cassock (French *casaque*) over the skimpy doublet, and in the 1650s it was frequently made to match with doublet and breeches. In the late 1670s it was narrowed and smartened to become the coat of a suit.

Caul A close-fitting, coif-like head-covering reaching to the nape of the neck behind, covering the ears, and framing the cheeks. Made from an open-work netting of silk, gold or silver thread or metal-work, it was frequently jewelled and finished with a deep ornamental border set with gem-stones. Usually it was lined with silk or cloth of gold. In this form it was worn by women during the second half of the 15th

[1] *See* Norah Waugh *The Cut of Men's Clothes*, pp. 28–29.

century on into the first quarter of the 16th. The same name was applied to a similarly netted cap worn from c. 1560–c. 1610 which covered only the plaits of hair coiled on to the back of the head.

Chaperon   A formalization of the turban formed from the hood. It was fashionable c. 1420–c. 1470, then was relegated to ceremonial wear being worn not on the head but hanging behind on the shoulder-blade. A miniature version of it survives on the shoulder of the robes of the Order of the Garter. It consisted of three parts: (1) The roundlet, a thick padded ring fitting on to the head. (2) The gorget, a flat circle of fabric with a hole in the centre. This was stitched into the roundlet, all the fullness falling to one side. (3) The liripipe, now made quite wide and very long. It was stitched into one side of the roundlet and was draped across the chest, then thrown over the opposite shoulder like a scarf.

Chasuble   A funnel-shaped outer cloak seamed together, leaving only a hole for the head. Derived from the Roman paenula, a utilitarian travelling garment, it was adopted as the most important liturgical garment of the early Christian Church, but was still in common use by laity as well as clergy as late as the 6th century.

Circassian or **circassienne**   A variant of the polonaise to which it is almost identical, its distinguishing feature being very short cap sleeves (sometimes fur edged) from inside which narrow wrist-length sleeves emerge. It was fashionable c. 1775–c. 1780. The title was probably suggested by the Turkish mania of the period, the sleeves somewhat resembling those of Turkish national dress.

Clavi Purple bands, running vertically from shoulder to hem, on the tunics of Roman dignitaries. Their number (one or two) and their width were originally indicative of rank, but like all such distinctions they tended to lose their initial symbolism and became ornamental.

Codpiece A triangular gusset used from about 1408 to cover the gap in front between the separate legs of the hose. The word 'cod' is both an old term for a bag, and a slang word for the testicles. By the 1490s padding was added, and from *c.* 1515 the codpiece became very prominent. It disappeared from fashionable dress *c.* 1575.

Coif A close-fitting linen bonnet tied under the chin (rather like a baby's bonnet). It was worn by men from the late 12th century until about the middle of the 15th; after that time it became a mark of the professional classes or the old-fashioned. It could be worn with any other type of headgear. A similar form of headgear was worn by women in the late 16th and early 17th centuries when it was generally richly embroidered in black-work (q.v.), white-work or coloured silks.

Commode Strictly the term applied to the wire frame supporting the **fontange** between *c.* 1690–*c.* 1710, but was sometimes used for the fontange itself. This was a cap made to fit over the coiled back hair, edged with a frill or frills of lace, which between *c.* 1690–*c.* 1700 were extended very high above the top of the head in front and intermixed with stiffened ribbon loops. Sometimes it rose vertical, but more usually leaned forward at an angle of about 45°. It had two long lace-edged streamers or lappets attached at the sides towards the back. The name fontange is reputedly derived from that of Mlle de Fontange (a mistress of Louis XIV) who is said to have invented this form of head-dress. In fact it is a logical development from a small close lace cap surmounted by a top-knot of ribbons worn on the back of the head from *c.* 1670. The 'Ladies Dictionary' of 1694 refers to the 'Font-Ange' as 'a modish Top-knot' and does not imply the whole head-dress. The complete erection of cap, commode and ribbon loops was generally called a 'head' at the time.

Contouche One variant on the loose *robes-de-chambres* fashionable *c.* 1710–*c.* 1730. They were of extremely simple construction, belonging to the same genus as the mantua, sack, etc.

Cote-hardie A close-fitting garment of the coat genus (i.e. opening down the front from neck to hem), it appeared first about 1325. At this time it was cut from four pieces (two fronts and two backs) moulded closely to the torso to just below the waist, from there flaring into a fuller skirt by the addition of gores. In length it reached – for men – to just above or just below the knee. The neck was cut into a low *bateau* shape, and the tight sleeves finished usually at the elbow with a pendant flap. It buttoned or laced from neck to fork and was from there left unfastened to the hem. After about 1350 the skirt was shortened and made narrower and it was then buttoned to its full length. Worn over the doublet it appeared usually in conjunction with a short caped hood covering the shoulders. Very quickly adopted by women for whom it was almost identical to the masculine garment, moulding the torso to the hips, and then flaring into a wide skirt trailing well on to the floor. Like the male garment its front fastening of buttons or lacing extended from a low *bateau* neck to about the fork, but from there to the hem it was seamed together. Some examples show no front fastening but were probably laced on each side from armpit to hip. The female version frequently had front 'fitchets' or pocket-holes – two vertical slits at hip level. The male cote-hardie ceased to be fashionable after *c.* 1415, but it was worn by women, particularly as ceremonial dress, until *c.* 1500. During the early 15th century the female version was sometimes made with wide sleeves like those of the houppelande.

Cravat A linen or muslin neck-scarf worn by men fashionably from *c.* 1665–*c.* 1730, and appearing until quite late in the 18th century. At first quite short, the scarf was placed around the neck over the collar-band of the shirt, and its two ends tied together under the chin by a bow of silk ribbon. From the 1690s onwards the cravat was frequently long, knotted at the throat, and the ends twisted together to fill the opening when the waistcoat was left unbuttoned on the breast. This version, called the 'Steinkirk cravat', was sometimes adopted by women during the 1690s.

Cul de Paris (False bum or false rump) A posterior pad or 'bustle' worn to support the draped-back skirt of the mantua *c.* 1680 until the reintroduction of a hooped petticoat *c.* 1710. Fashionable again (*culs postiches*) in the late 1770s–*c.* 1800, when they were sometimes made from cork.

Cuts A means of adding decorative effect to textiles, much used in the 16th and early 17th centuries, was the cutting of slits in the surface. These varied from ½in.–2 or 3 in. (12.7mm–5 or 8cm) in length and were made on the diagonal of the weave, arranged in patterned formations. It was rare for the cut to be finished around the edge, so that in a loosely woven fabric fringing would automatically appear. There is no documentary evidence for the exact method employed to produce the cuts. As some cuts are serrated these would suggest the use of a specially shaped chisel-like instrument, and the existence of buttonhole chisels also points to this method, but there seems to be no total agreement among authorities.

Dalmatic A long wide-sleeved tunic worn as an outer garment in late Roman times (1st–5th centuries). Supposedly oriental in origin, it appears to have been made at first exclusively from white Dalmatian wool. Adopted as an ecclesiastical vestment by the early Christian Church.

Doublet A fitted garment of the coat genus (opening down the centre front from neck to hem). In origin it appears to have been an insulation to prevent the chafing of the skin by metal armour (the **arming-doublet**). Being wadded or padded all over it was worn *as* armour by rank and file soldiers and was the work of 'linen armourers'. In this guise it appears under various names – gambeson; gipon; jupon; etc. It was adopted as a civilian foundation garment *c.* 1325 onwards. At first cut in four sections (two fronts and two backs), it was very closely fitted, extending to mid-thigh, and had close wrist-length sleeves. It fastened by lacing or buttoning down the centre front – the sleeves also being laced or buttoned either for their full length or from elbow to wrist. For fashionable wear it was interlined with wadding (except for a narrow section down the centre back) held in place by quilting or stab-stitching. Its Italian name – *farsetto* – derives from *farsa* (any kind of stuffing) and the quilters were called *farsettai*. Outside fashionable circles it does not appear to have been padded and quilted but only lined with a thick, fleecy, blanket-like fabric. To it the hose were trussed, at first by tapes stitched inside its lower edge, later by 'points' or laces passed through eyelet-holes worked into the skirt to correspond with similar eyelets in the top edge of the hose. It was covered *c.* 1325–*c.* 1470 by the cote-hardie, later by some variant of the houppelande, showing only the collar and on the forearm. By *c.* 1460 it was being cut in eight body sections, having acquired a waist seam to prevent wrinkling. The skirts were gradually shortened throughout the second half of the 15th century until by the 1490s it was waist length. The fashion for wearing the doublet without any over-garment began at about this time in Italy and was quickly adopted all over Europe. From *c.* 1500–*c.* 1660 it was the principal upper garment, only sometimes covered by a jerkin, and generally by a gown or cloak. Its variations may be followed in the illustrations from pp. 58–89 until it was relegated to a kind of waistcoat *c.* 1662 under a coat. Almost immediately it was replaced by the vest.

Dundrearies Exaggeratedly long side whiskers fashionable in the 1860s and '70s and named after a character – Lord Dundreary – played by the actor E. A. Sothern in Tom Taylor's *Our American Cousin* in 1861. They were also known as 'Piccadilly Weepers'.

Echelle Originally the ribbons tied in bows to close

the front of the mantua when it first appeared *c.* 1676. Later formalized into a series of made-up, graduated bows to decorate the stomacher and continuing in fashion from *c.* 1690–*c.* 1770.

Engageantes Lace ruffles falling out from the elbow-length sleeves of a woman's mantua or gown from the 1690s. At first attached to the sleeve of the shift they were later made up as separate items by the modiste and tacked into the gown sleeve. They were usually made in two or three layers and became very deep, almost covering the lower arm in the mid-18th century.

Farthingale A shaped under-skirt of fabric held out into a smooth cone by a graduated series of flexible rods of cane, whalebone, or similar stiffeners, bent into hoops and inserted into casings attached to the garment. The name is an English derivation from the Spanish *verdugado*. The word *verdugos* means a young sapling, from which the rods were probably originally taken. Garments framed out smoothly by this means were seen in northern Spain from *c.* 1460 and gradually infiltrated into fashionable dress, possibly by way of exotic masquing costume. They became general to Europe *c.* 1540 in the cone-shaped, or Spanish farthingale, which remained fashionable (varied slightly from cone to bell shape) until *c.* 1590. Although surviving in an exaggerated form until *c.* 1660, or even later, in Spain and areas under Spanish dominion (i.e. parts of Italy, etc.), its popularity in France and England was superseded *c.* 1590 by another type, now called the French farthingale. This was a circle or oval of fabric, framed out by rods, extending only from waist to hip level. The skirt worn over it dropped straight from the edge to the floor. In its extreme form it was mainly for ceremonial or formal wear, being replaced by a bum-roll for general wear. This type of farthingale was fashionable *c.* 1590–*c.* 1615.

Fontange, *see* **Commode**

Frock   This word has had various meanings at different times. It was used in the 16th century for a loose over-garment, and in the 18th century was first used for a man's riding coat, cut (though not to our eyes) rather loose fitting, and having as its most distinctive feature a turn-down collar – unlike the formal coat which had no collar, or else a narrow standing band. It was later applied to the loose garments worn by children *c.* 1760 onwards, and by grown women *c.* 1780–*c.* 1800, which were cut with body and skirt in one piece and gathered on a draw-string at neck and waist. Its association with a loose over-garment was retained in the 'smock-frock' worn by farm labourers in the late 18th–early 19th centuries and onwards. After 1800 the term was rather loosely applied to any female dress.

Frock-coat   This is distinguished from the masculine 'frock' of the 18th century by having skirts cut evenly all round at about (or just below) knee level, instead of being sloped away in a curve in front or cut back square at the waist leaving only tails behind. This new type of frock-coat appeared first in the late 1790s, being worn by the more extreme and raffish 'Incroyables' in the wild period following the Terror. It came into general fashion *c.* 1815 and became the most usual formal coat for the whole of the 19th century, being worn by the conservative well into the 20th. It varied enormously in style during its period of popularity, being made single or double breasted; with full skirts or narrow; with broad revers or very small ones, sometimes silk faced. It could have a velvet collar, and was sometimes edged with silk braid. It was made with a centre-back vent and its pocket was concealed inside the back lining of the coat, accessible only by putting the hand into the vent. The buttons generally stopped at the waist where the garment was seamed, leaving the front skirts unfastened, and usually there were narrow pleats in the skirt at the back, on each side of the vent, finished by a button at the top, placed at waist level.

Frogging An ornamentation made from horizontally applied bands of braid or cord marking the buttonholes and corresponding button-placings. Usually finished at the outer point by a tassel or tuft. In origin Turkish or Near Eastern, and introduced into Europe when the kaftan was adopted as a house-robe by both men and women in the 16th century. It appeared particularly on men's coats and vests *c.* 1680 to continue in popularity, on and off, throughout the 18th and early 19th centuries. Much used on military uniform, when it could be very elaborate. Such military frogging was used on civilian garments (particularly top-coats) during times of strong influence from the army – as during the Napoleonic régime and the war which followed.

Galloon A ribbon-like trimming of closely worked but lacy texture in silk or metal thread, variable in width from about ¼in. (6.3mm) to as much as 2 or 3in. (5 or 8 cm). (French *galon*). In the 17th century it was much used on both male and female dress –

particularly for the elaborate banding of a woman's gown and petticoat, and also to mark the buttonholes and button-placings on a man's coat and vest.

Garnache, *see* **Surcoat**

Gore A section of fabric cut to an elongated triangular shape, used for adding width to the hem of a skirt when it is not desirable to have pleats or gathers at the waist. In its simplest form two gores were set into each side of the straight front and back sections of a tunic in the Middle Ages. This gives an unaesthetic appearance since all fullness is concentrated at the sides leaving the centre front and back to hang in a rather 'dead' way. A more pleasing appearance is given if the gores are evenly distributed, and an elegantly cut skirt of the late 1890s may be composed from as many as seven to nine gored sections.

Gown A term which has changed its meaning several times. Strictly it is a sleeved outer garment of the coat genus (opening in front from neck to hem). Originally the word seems to have been used only for loosely fitting full-length garments. Later used to include not only those of any length, but also those with a closely fitted body and wide skirts – thus in the 18th century the term was used as an alternative to mantua (as was the word 'robe') and so gradually came to be applied to almost any feminine dress (as in the 20th century 'Gown-shop'). During the 15th and 16th centuries, however, its use was much more clearly defined. It was after *c.* 1450 that the word took over from the earlier houppelande, when this masculine outer garment was beginning on occasion to be left unfastened at the front (partly or completely) to display the doublet and hose beneath. By the late 15th century the rigid formality of the pleated houppelande had softened into a flaring, pleated, but unpadded garment, with wide revers and collar, always worn open in front. In this form (but with many variations of length and sleeves) it lasted as the principal male (and frequently female) outer garment until *c.* 1560. At about this time the masculine form for full-dress began to fossilize. The gown began to be made with flat dummy sleeves, and so was gradually transformed into a cloak. For undress-wear gowns continued in their earlier, loose, coat-like shape – usually floor-length and often with hanging-sleeves (attached only at the armsceye and not seamed vertically to cover the arm). From *c.* 1560 the feminine gown also went through a transformation, beginning to be made with a fitted body and full skirt (gored or pleated from the waist). It was almost always open in front to display the underlying bodice or stomacher and the petticoat. The loose house-gown with hanging-sleeves was also retained by women, and both forms, fitted and unfitted, continued in use until *c.* 1625 or later – gradually to re-emerge *c.* 1675 as the mantua. The 15th and 16th century masculine forms have been retained as distinctive ceremonial wear to mark the various degrees of scholarship, and also by barristers, judges, etc. The term 'robe' has a parallel history and has always been used indiscriminately as an alternative to gown.

Guild regulations   From the Middle Ages until the end of the 18th century most craft workers were members of craft guilds. These were a kind of trade union – a safeguard for the workers' jobs and conditions of labour, and also a means of setting standards of excellence, since a 'master-piece' had to be approved before a worker was fully accepted by the guild masters. The enforcement of guild regulations in the limiting of work only to guild members was variable from country to country, and probably from area to area, but to some extent they did exercise restraint over which particular workers could produce specific articles, and the standards to which these articles must conform. This did not therefore provide an atmosphere conducive to innovation and the regulations were possibly one factor accounting for the slow development of dress, its conservatism and uniformity, until the end of the 18th century.

Hennin A tall steeple-shaped head-dress fashionable at the courts of France and Burgundy c. 1460–80 often covered by a long flowing veil or by arrangements of stiffened and wired veils rising above it. It was worn high on the crown of the head and tilted backwards, the front hair being shaved. It was never fashionable in its extreme form elsewhere in Europe, but truncated versions, rather like an inverted flower-pot, were worn in England, Germany and in north Italy.

Hessian boot A boot worn with pantaloons c. 1795–c. 1830. Its distinctive characteristic is the line at the top, curving round the calf behind but rising to a sharp point to just below the knee in front (where it is sometimes curved into a cupid's-bow form). The top edge is decorated by a narrow band of contrasting leather or metallic braid and there is a pendant tassel from the front point. It continues to form a part of some military dress uniforms.

Hose Literally stockings, a covering for the feet extending upwards over the lower leg generally reaching to above the knee. But their development and history is complex. Although knitting was known to the Ancient Egyptians, who had used the process to make socks, and although circular knitting on four pins was practised during the Middle Ages, knitted hose were very rare. Possibly the home-made stockings *were* knitted, but fashionable hose were of woven fabric cut on the bias. They appear first during the 9th century, worn by men, who pulled them up over the long trouser-like braies to hold these close to the lower leg, as an alternative to leg-bandages. They do not appear to have been fastened, and they wrinkled loosely below the knee. From about the 12th century they were made much longer, and the natural point on the thigh which is left when a rectangle of woven fabric is wrapped around the leg on the true bias (that is, with the warp and weft threads crossing the centred vertical line of the leg at an angle of exactly 45°) was fastened by a cord or tape to the draw-string of the braies (*see* **Braies**). The bias-cut hose had only one seam at the centre back of the leg. From the mid-14th century the hose were lengthened again so that the top (at thigh level) could be cut evenly all round, and into the top edge eyelet-holes were worked, enabling the hose to be supported by tapes stitched inside the hem of the doublet, these being passed through the eyelets and knotted. A little later the fastening was made by separate points (laces with a metal tag at each end), which were inserted into eyelet-holes worked in the doublet hem to correspond with those at the top of the hose. The operation of uniting the three pieces (doublet and two stockings) was known as 'trussing the points'. The bias-cut hose were unlined, except for a linen facing about 3in. (8cm) deep around the top edge to strengthen the fabric for working the eyelets. But fastidious people wore them over linen socks or under-stockings. Until well after 1400 it was unusual for the stockings to be joined at the seat, so that when over-garments were removed the linen under-drawers were visible at seat and crotch. But from *c.* 1400, when extremely short clothes became the fashion, some hose were stitched together at the seat to form tights, and the front opening was covered by a movable gusset – the codpiece. From *c.* 1500 attention concentrated on the thigh which began to be much decorated with applied ornament or with cuts, and the hose were then often made in two colours and fabrics, joined together at about mid-thigh. These were **upper-** and **nether-stocks**. The nether-stocks began sometimes to be knitted from the early 1550s, but were still stitched to the upper-stocks. These upper-stocks increased in complexity after 1550, being gradually distended to enormous padded pumpkin-like forms by 1565, cut into strips (panes) through which full interlinings were pulled. From this time styles were of extreme variety. During the 1580s knitted hose were generally made to rise only a little above the knee, being gartered below it. The gap between these shorter hose and the short upper-stocks (or **trunk-hose**, i.e. that part of the hose nearest the trunk) being filled by canions. After *c.* 1625 hose became stockings as they are still known today. Female hose had never been made to rise higher than just above the knee, and were gartered below it until the 19th century.

Houppelande The term derives from the Spanish *hoppalanda* (a tunic) which, with its form, would seem to indicate an Arabic origin. It was a bell-shaped garment, fitted at the shoulder, and flaring from there to an enormous circumference at the hem, which was at first generally floor-length. It had very wide funnel-shaped sleeves, reaching the wrist on top, but descending in a deep point to the floor at the back. Usually it had a very high close collar and was fastened in front by buttons, lacing or hooks and eyes, from neck to fork. In this form it became fashionable for both men and women *c.* 1375. When worn by men it was often left open on the side seams or front and back seams from hem to knee level. Men belted the fullness at waist or hip level – women always immediately beneath the bust. By *c.* 1400 shorter variations were worn by men, anywhere from calf length to as short as the hip-bones. After *c.* 1440 the fullness was pulled to front and back and stitched into symmetrical 'organ-pipe' pleats, leaving the sides plain. After *c.* 1450 it became the 'gown' for men. When worn by women, the collar was left open falling flat on to the shoulders from *c.* 1410, and it was gradually developed into a gown with a deep V-necked opening bordered by revers by *c.* 1440. In this form it lasted until the end of the 15th century.

Jerkin In origin this over-garment was a cross between the cote-hardie and the short houppelande. It was worn over the doublet from *c.* 1450, being generally called the 'jacket' until *c.* 1500. During the 15th century it was almost identical to the short houppelande, with formal pleats drawn to centre front and back and stitched into position. After *c.* 1500 it was usually made with a fitted body exactly covering the doublet, and with full skirts set on in pleats at the waist. From *c.* 1540 the skirts were generally plain and gradually shortened to reveal the upper-stocks. By *c.* 1550 the skirts were short enough to appear like a narrow basque, and had by *c.* 1560 been reduced to a narrow scalloped border. By this date it is almost indistinguishable from the doublet over which it was worn, but, being generally sleeveless or with hanging sleeves, revealed the doublet itself on the arms. It was replaced by the cassock or coat during the 1650s.

Kirtle This was the fitted foundation garment for women after *c.* 1330, and was the equivalent of the male doublet, although it was not padded or quilted. Cut with curved seams, it was made to mould closely to the torso down to hip level and from there spread in flaring folds to the floor. It laced or buttoned from a *bateau* neck to about the fork in front, or laced on each side from armpit to hip. Like the male doublet, it had long tight sleeves buttoning or lacing from elbow to wrist, or sometimes the full length of the arm. It was worn over the shift and was generally covered by a cote-hardie or a houppelande, as was the masculine doublet. The kirtle was worn by working women with no over-garment and then often had very short sleeves allowing the shift to show, falling to the wrist. When 'dressed', the woman could add long sleeves (often of a different fabric) pinned or tied by points to the short sleeve of the kirtle.

Liripipe A long narrow length of fabric seamed into a tube and pressed flat to form a narrow ribbon-like band. This was attached as a pendant to the point of the hood from *c.* 1330. After the hood had formalized into the chaperon, the liripipe was often made like a long wide scarf (its edges sometimes cut into petal or leaf shapes) stitched into one side of the roundlet (*see* **Chaperon**).

Mancheron An early technical term about which there is dispute. In the present text it has been used in its 19th century definition of a cape-like half-sleeve falling from the shoulder to about elbow level.

Mantle An alternative name for a cloak. In early times it could be rectangular, but after the 12th century was generally circular or semi-circular. Sometimes it had a hood attached to it, and occasionally slits on each side to allow the arms to pass through. Generally it fastened only at the neck by a brooch or by tasselled cords. The name continued in use into the early 20th century, many large stores having a department called 'Cloaks and mantles'.

Mantua An English corruption of the French *manteau*. In origin a loose, unfitted, dressing-gown, worn only in the privacy of the home. After *c.* 1675 it began to be worn as an 'undress' garment in public over corset and petticoat and was then made to fit closely to the body by stitching the fullness in pleats to waist level. It formed the basis for all the variations of the main female dress or robe of the 18th century, being either sack-backed or close-backed according to taste and fashion. It was important as being the first main garment (as opposed to underwear) made by women for women instead of by a male tailor, and the mantua-maker was the ancestress of the dressmaker.

Mob-cap An 'undress' cap with a very deep puffed crown and frilled border, the join between the two being usually marked by a ribbon. It became fashionable about 1730 and continued throughout the 18th century, becoming very exaggerated in the 1770s and '80s when it was often worn in conjunction with a wide brimmed hat. In more modest versions it was the regular wear for servants.

Modiste The supplier and/or applier of the elaborate trimming and accessories to 18th century female dress. Working on the simple regular basis of whalebone body or corset, petticoat and robe or mantua, the modiste would add decoration of lace, ruching, ribbons, cords, tassels, artificial flowers, etc., giving each ensemble its individual distinction, and so is the true ancestor of the *couturier* in the sense in which that word is now used (i.e. the designer of a dress). Rose Bertin (one of the first well-known names among the creators of fashionable dress) was modiste to Marie Antoinette, and appears mainly to have trimmed rather than made the royal garments.

Nankeen An Indian cotton textile of a brownish-yellow 'natural' colour much used for men's trousers in the early 19th century.

Paenula A semi-circular piece of fabric made into a closed, funnel-shaped outer garment by seaming it together at the front, leaving only a vertical slit at the top for the head to pass through. Usually a folded rectangle of fabric was stitched to the edges of this slit to form a hood. The resulting hooded cape was worn by shepherds and travellers, and for extra covering by both men and women throughout Europe under the Roman empire. It could be of any length, but was usually either to about mid-calf or to the elbow. The direct ancestor of the ecclesiastical chasuble, it became also, fashionably, the caped secular hood of the 14th century.

Palla A rectangular cloak or wrapped garment, in width about the same measurement as the wearer from shoulder to foot, and some three times as long. It was the outdoor garment of the Roman woman, as the toga was that of the man.

Pallium A rectangular cloak or wrapped garment identical with the female palla, but worn by Roman scholars and philosophers, sometimes as the only garment.

Panes The trunk-hose, or upper-stocks, worn by men between *c.* 1500 and *c.* 1600, were generally made decorative by being cut vertically from waistband to base every 2–3in. (5–8cm), allowing a much more fully gathered interlining to puff through the slits. This was called 'paning' the garment – hence 'panes' are the cuts. As an alternative, the trunk-hose might be made from separate strips of fabric joined to the waistband above and to another narrow band at the base, but the finished effect would be that of paned breeches.

Pantaloons A transitional form between knee-breeches and trousers fashionable between *c.* 1790 and *c.* 1825–30. Like knee-breeches they were cut skin-tight with fall-front closures, but like trousers they covered at least part of the lower leg, ending variably between the base of the calf and the top of the ankle-bone. Worn at a time when waistcoats were short, they were cut very high in the rise, reaching above the waist to the lower ribs and so required support from shoulder braces. They buttoned or laced on the lower leg and were often worn tucked inside knee-high or Hessian boots. Frequently of soft leather, they were also made from silk stockinet.

Parti-colouring   A parti-coloured garment is one in which the various sections from which it is composed are made from fabric of different colours. For example, the left front may be red and the right front blue, the right back red and the left back blue, so that the two colours alternate around the body. This system was highly fashionable from the late 12th–early 15th centuries, but was continued even into the early 16th century on occasions. It could assume great complexity during the late 14th century when bodies, sleeves, hoods and hose could all be made up from many pieces, the colouring carefully arranged to emphasize the parts by contrast. The cote-hardies worn by both men and women and the woman's sideless-surcoat were particularly treated in this way. Originating as a useful military device, for speedy identification of the factions on a battlefield, it was first seen in the surcoat or tabard worn over armour, and the colours would be those associated with a particular family. Such parti-colouring was worn also as livery by an over-lord's civilian servants and retainers. By the 14th century parti-colouring had become high fashion and had lost much of its earlier symbolism, although its use as livery in the family colours was continued for another century, and on rare occasions even longer.

Patches   Small pieces of black fabric – spots, crescents, stars, etc. – glued to the face, neck or breast, and much used in fashionable circles during the 17th and 18th centuries. Possibly ornamental in origin; but there is some evidence that they were used to cover scars left from the pox or other skin blemishes.

Peascod-belly This fashion for padding out the stomach of a man's doublet until it resembled the base of a pea-pod when seen in profile appeared about 1560. At that time it was little more than the form given by the extreme stiffness of the buttoned front edges of the garment, but the effect was gradually exaggerated to reach an extreme by *c*. 1580–1585. By then really fashionable doublets could be made with a thickly padded, 'hard-quilted' paunch drooping over the waistband to reach as low as the fork. This form of doublet is the traditional wear for Punch in the Punch and Judy show, having its origin in the costume worn by Pulcinella, one of the stock characters in the Italian Commedia dell'Arte. After *c*. 1585 the exaggerated forms gradually disappeared, but examples of a moderate kind continued (unfashionably) into the early 17th century.

Pelisse A woman's top-coat *c*. 1800–*c*. 1830, made on the same lines as the fashionable dress but fastening all down the front. Often made with capes as well as a collar.

Peplum Originally derived from the Ancient Greek *peplos* – a rectangle of cloth with the top folded over and pinned on the shoulders, giving the appearance of a short skirted bodice worn over a long skirt. During the Neo-classical revival of the late 18th–early 19th centuries short over-skirts were gathered on at the waist of fitted bodices to suggest the ancient garment.

Periwig This term appears to have been an early corruption of the word 'peruke', meaning a tight cap covered with hair so as to resemble a natural growth.

Its usage is now generally reserved for the profuse and heavy arrangements of massed hair hanging in thick clumps on to each shoulder in front, and falling sometimes as low as the waist behind, which were fashionable for men between *c.* 1660 and *c.* 1715. The word was, however, used to denote any form of wig from the late 16th century onwards, and was contracted to 'wig' by the 18th century, at the time when the periwig itself was being reduced in volume.

Pet en l'air   One of the many informal jacket-like bodices worn by women as 'undress' between *c.* 1745 and *c.* 1775. It was like a shortened sack-back mantua, ending anywhere between mid-thigh to hip length. Very fashionable in the 1750s.

Petticoat-breeches, *see* **Breeches**

Plastic ornament   A form of decoration used on the fronts of the open-skirted robe or mantua, and the petticoat beneath, during the 1770s. It consisted of ovals or other abstract shapes of the dress fabric, slightly gathered around the edges to make them puff up, and then laid over soft wadding. Usually the sections were edged with narrow braid, cord, or lace, and arranged in serpentine or zigzag chains down the skirt fronts and in horizontal bands across the petticoat.

Pocket-holes   During the 18th century a woman's pockets were not stitched into the skirt but were made like two flat bags to hang one on each hip, suspended from a tape tied about the waist underneath the hoop, petticoat and robe, hence each of these garments had to have a slit left on each side to allow access to the pockets themselves. The pocket-holes in the mantua were of importance fashionably since it was a general practice on informal occasions (and also among servants) to truss the skirt in the pocket-holes. To do this the two front corners of the mantua were turned inwards and pulled up through the pocket-holes, thus drawing the skirt into a draped swag behind. From this practice it is possible that inspiration was given for the formalized trussing of the skirt in the polonaise and circassienne.

Polonaise An informal dress highly fashionable *c.* 1775–80. Its principal characteristic was that the skirt was drawn up to form three large puffs or swags, one on each hip and one centrally behind. This was achieved in various ways: either by drawing the skirt up on internal cords which ran through a series of rings stitched to the inside of the side-back seams; or by loops of cord stitched inside the waist which were passed over a button on the outside waist; or by a ribbon stitched inside being tied in a bow to a corresponding ribbon outside. The polonaise was cut in its general principle like a mantua, and could be close-bodied or sack-backed. It was also in appearance very similar to the circassienne, the only difference being in the form of the sleeves, those of the polonaise being elbow-length, and in trimming following the modes used for decorating the mantua. There was a revival of over-tunic skirts during the 1870s and some tea-gowns were made in a form almost identical to the polonaise of the 18th century.

Reticule Sometimes called 'ridicule', it was a variety of hand-bag introduced during the 1790s when the soft muslins and scanty volume of the most fashionable female dress made the wearing of the traditional bag pockets beneath the robe impossible. Usually made from satin, or some other textile, they were simple bags closed by gathering cords slotted through the top, and suspended from the wrist by ribbons.

Robe volante One term for the very loose, négligé garments worn by women during the first thirty to forty years of the 18th century. Very simply constructed, they had fullness laid in pleats across the back and shoulders which spread out over the wide domed hoop petticoats worn beneath.

Robings The turn-back or revers on each side of the open bodice of the woman's mantua or robe in the 18th century. They began from a straight band across the nape, came forward over the shoulders and reached to just below the waistline, although they could be carried through to the full length of the skirt. After about 1745 they were sometimes made as a separate item, like a U-shaped collar, the centre of the U behind, pinned around the open front of the bodice, and finishing at the waist or an inch or two below.

Ruff, *see* **Band**

Sack or **sacque** Usually applied from the 17th century onwards to any loose négligé garment worn by a woman. A sack-backed gown was one in which fullness was laid across the shoulders in pleats stitched down only for a few inches at the shoulder-blades and then left to flow freely into the fullness of the skirt.

Shift The principal piece of female underwear throughout history from the earliest times until the 19th century. Sometimes called the 'smock'. It was essentially a tunic, being wide and loose without fastening and slipped on over the head. Until the 17th century it generally had long narrowish sleeves – after that elbow-length sleeves with ruffles of lace or white-work (*see* **Black-work**) to finish them. Very like a night-dress, its length usually went to about mid-calf. It was the female version of the man's shirt.

Slashing   A method of adding interest to dress, very prevalent during the 16th and early 17th centuries. It consisted of long, generally vertical, cuts made on the breast, back and sleeves of body garments, and on hose, allowing the under-garment to show, or an extra full lining to puff out between. The mode appeared briefly again, but modified, during the early 1800s as a romantic revival, mostly on the sleeves of women's dresses and spencers.

Spangles   Small discs, ovals, or raindrop-shaped pieces of very thin sparkling metal, pierced with a hole so that they could be sewn to the surface of the fabric. Much used from the second half of the 16th century onwards as a trimming for the clothes of both men and women, they were often combined with metallic lace or embroidery to give this extra glitter. The drop-shaped pieces, attached only at the top, were used to finish lace fringes and borders, flashing as they dangled freely from the edges. Sometimes when the centre holes were large they were called 'oes', and sometimes 'sequins', taking this name from a Venetian gold coin.

Spencer   A very short top-coat or jacket having no tails. It was worn by men during the 1790s as an extra covering over the tailed coat or frock, which hung below. It had long sleeves and was frequently decorated with military-style frogging. Said to have been invented by Earl Spencer who singed the tails of his coat when standing before a fire and had them trimmed off. A female version was very popular in the early 19th century, cut very short and reaching only just below the bust.

Stock A neck-band of linen or cambric worn by men from *c.* 1735 onwards in place of a neck-cloth or cravat. It was usually fully gathered or folded, horizontally, on to a narrow base and fastened behind with a tab and buckle. It was worn over the narrow standing collar of the shirt, which buttoned together in front, and left the lace ruffle outlining the front slit of the shirt to show below. Made exaggeratedly wide, rising up to the chin and ears during the 1790s, it continued in more or less this form until about 1820, then declined in popularity. With this deep stock the starched shirt collar also increased in height and its pointed corners rested on the cheeks just above the top edge of the stock.

Stocks, Upper- and **nether-**, *see* **Hose**

Stomacher A term used in the 15th century for a false front worn by men under the deeply cut-away opening of the doublet. It was also applied to any band, or triangular-shaped false front inserted into the opening of a woman's dress from the 15th–18th centuries. Generally mounted on some stiffened foundation, it was usually elaborately decorated with embroidery, ribbon bows, etc., and was pinned to the corset or whalebone body beneath the robe.

Surcoat This term was applied to a wide variety of outer garments worn by both men and women from the 13th century until the word 'gown' began to replace it during the 15th century. Usually the surcoat was of the tunic genus, that is, made loose enough to be slipped on over the head and not cut to fit closely to the body. Frequently sleeveless, the surcoat could be of any length between knee level and the floor, although it was general for it to be made slightly shorter than the main garment so that this would show below. It could be slit from hem to hip level either in front or on each side. If it had sleeves these were loose and wide and usually shorter than those of the under-garment, finishing about half-way down the forearm. Alternatively, the sleeves could be very long, having a slit at elbow level through which the arm could be passed to leave the rest of the sleeve hanging as a loose, wide tube. Particular variants in the 13th and 14th centuries were the garde-corps (with very long, fully gathered tubular sleeves, vertically slit on the front seam for the passage of the arm, and equipped with a hood) and the **garnache** (the upper part cut into wide, semi-circular cape-sleeves falling to elbow level). Many surcoats had fitchets or pocket-holes on each side of the centre front at waist or hip level to allow access to the purse carried on the belt beneath. The female sideless gown of the 14th and 15th centuries was another development of the surcoat.

Tabard A sleeveless garment seamed only at the shoulders, and hanging in loose panels on chest and back. Being open at the sides, it allowed any garment worn beneath to be visible. It was sometimes belted at the waist or hip, or the belt would be passed over the front section only, leaving the back panel to hang free like a cloak. Fashionable for men, on and off, from the 13th–15th centuries. Retained later as part of heraldic and military formal costume, the coat of arms generally being embroidered on front and back.

Tablion A rectangular patch of elaborate embroidery, worked generally on to cloth of gold, and applied to the front and back edges of the Byzantine semi-circular court cloak, which was worn fastened on the right shoulder, so that the tablion lay on the front edge from chest to fork, and on the back edge from shoulder-blade to buttocks. It appeared mainly between the 5th and 10th centuries A.D., worn by emperors and nobles, but from the 8th–11th centuries it was also worn by empresses.

Templers Cases of silk-net richly decorated, or of metal goldsmiths' work, covering the plaited and coiled hair of women during the 15th century. They were worn above the ears, and projected sideways and slightly forward over each temple. Generally they were covered by veils (wired or not) or by a padded roll bent into a heart shape, or by a variant of the masculine chaperon. Noble ladies wore them surmounted by specially oval-shaped coronets.

Toga An outer wrap worn by Roman citizens. Originally quite small in size, it seems to have been shaped to the segment of a circle, and was decorated on the curved edge. From the 1st century B.C.–5th century A.D., it was increased to vast proportions and was draped and folded in a variety of complicated ways, growing ever more formal as time went on. The band of decoration on this later toga was applied to the straight edge. For ordinary wear it was of wool in its natural colour and undecorated, but the toga praetexta, worn by youths under sixteen and by magistrates, had a band of plain purple or scarlet. There were other symbolic decorations for particularly prescribed occasions.

Trunk-hose, *see* **Hose**

Tunic The earliest and simplest *shaped* but not *fitted* garment. It was originally in essentials a straight tube of woven fabric with lateral extensions at right angles on each side at the top to form sleeves. This basic T-shaped garment was the Roman tunica. Later, given the addition of triangular gores at each side, to widen it from waist to hem, it became the tunic of the early Middle Ages. Several tunics of different widths and lengths could be worn one over another, the outer ones being called super-tunics. Loose enough to slip on over the head, they had no fastening nor any distinctive shaping to limit their use to one sex.

Tweedside jacket A lounging jacket introduced for men's 'undress' wear about 1858. It was unwaisted, straight and loose, reaching to mid-thigh and single breasted. Made with a turn-down collar and short revers, it was usually worn buttoned only at the top and left to hang loose. It was the ancestor of the modern suit-jacket, but was worn only for informal occasions until the end of the 19th century.

Under-propper A fan-shaped support of paste-board covered with silk, or of wire whipped with silk or metallic ribbon, used to hold up the very wide fashionable band or ruff of the late 1580s onwards. It was pinned to the collar of the doublet or bodice, and the starched ruff was then pinned to it.

Undress A term implying dress not intended for full ceremonial or gala wear, but yet retaining some marks of formality, as in the 'undress uniform' of a military regiment.

Venetians Knee-breeches introduced for men *c.* 1570 as an alternative to hose. Sometimes they were skin-tight and were topped by a padded hip-roll resembling a miniature version of trunk-hose. Usually they were fully gathered or pleated on to the waistband and narrowed towards the hem in a pear shape. In slight variations of this form they continued fashionable until about 1620.

Vest A close-fitting, thigh-length, sleeved under-coat or waistcoat which replaced the doublet *c.* 1662 or thereabouts, worn under a similarly cut, but slightly looser cassock. During the 18th century it became the waistcoat, although Americans and some English tailors still retain the term vest for this garment, even today.

Wimple A rectangle of linen used by women to cover the neck. It was placed under the chin, wrapped around the head and pinned to the coils of hair over the ears; the two ends overlapped behind and were pinned to the crown of the head. Its lower edge hung just on to the shoulders. Sometimes it was worn alone, allowing the centre-parted hair to show above, but more usually it was accompanied by a linen head-cloth or veil, so that only the face was visible in the V-shaped opening left between the two. It was fashionable during the 13th and early 14th centuries, thereafter being relegated to the use of the elderly, widows and members of religious orders.

Select Bibliography

History

Boucher, F., 1967. *A History of Costume in the West.* Thames and Hudson.

Davenport, M., 1964. *The Book of Costume.* Crown Publishers, New York.

Kybalová, L., Herbenova, O., and Lamorova, M., 1969. *The Pictorial Encyclopedia of Fashion.* Hamlyn.

Payne, B., 1965. *History of Costume.* Harper & Row, New York.

Theory

Bell, Q., 1947. *On Human Finery.* Hogarth Press.

Cunnington, C. W., 1948. *The Art of English Costume.* Collins.

Flügel, J. C., 1950. *The Psychology of Clothes.* Hogarth Press.

Hiler, H., 1929. *From Nudity to Raiment.* Simpkin Marshall.

Squire, G., 1974. *Dress, Art and Society.* Studio Vista.

Practice

Arnold, J., 1972. *Patterns of Fashion.* Macmillan.

Bradfield, N., 1968. *Costume in Detail.* Harrap.

Waugh, N., 1964. *The Cut of Men's Clothes.* Faber & Faber.

Waugh, N., 1968. *The Cut of Women's Clothes.* Faber & Faber.

Waugh, N., 1970. *Corsets and Crinolines.* Batsford.

Some Important Collections
of Costume

Great Britain

Bath. Museum of Costume
London. London Museum
London. Victoria and Albert Museum
Manchester (Platt Hall). Gallery of English Costume
Names and addresses of other British collections are
 listed in: Arnold, J., 1973. *A Handbook of Costume.*
 Macmillan.

Europe

Amsterdam. Rijksmuseum
Copenhagen. National Museum
Copenhagen. Rosenborg Castle
Oslo. Kunstindustrimuseet
Paris. Musée du Costume de la Ville de Paris
Paris. Union Française des Arts du Costume
Stockholm. The Royal Armoury and Nordiska
 Museet
Vienna (Castle Hetzendorf). Fashion Collection of the
 City of Vienna

Index

(All woven materials will be found under **textiles**)